ASCEND

from Paycheck to Prosperity

The Journ
from Financial
Stress and
Struggle to
Financial
Freedom and
Abundance

Dr. Juanita Taylor

ASCEND

from Paycheck to Prosperity

The Journey from Financial Stress and Struggle to Financial Freedom and Abundance

Published by Krystal Lee Enterprises (KLE Publishing)
 Please send comments and questions:

Krystal Lee Enterprises
770-240-0089 Ext. 1
sales@KLEPub.com

To Reach the Author:
Email: info@askdrjuanita.com

Web: www.askdrjuanita.com
Social Handle Facebook & Instagram: Ask Dr Juanita
Facebook Group: Women ASCENDing

Printed in the United States of America.

ISBN: **979-8-89987-901-2**

Dedication

I dedicate this book to my children, my grandchildren, my family, and my new family, my readers. My children are the reason for my drive, determination, dedication, and discipline. I want them to know that no matter what life throws your way, you must make a decision to continue beyond the uncertainties and pain-points of life.

It is because I continued on that I get to experience the high emotions on the other side of my shame, doubt, frustration, hurt, and fear. If I had given up, I could not explain the joy and peace that I experience now because I stayed the course. Not because I am better than anyone, but because I trusted God to order my steps when I could not see my way through my journey. You cannot and must not quit on yourself; under no circumstances.

There have been many days that I was afraid to move forward, but if I had not continued, I would not be here in this moment of realizing my dream of having a book that will be a ministry for many to read and experience. I choose to believe that many times God is grooming us for the very next thing he has for us in life. But if we cannot sustain what he has for us, he will not get us to our destiny and the promise that he has for us.

I encourage you to stay the course of your journey and know that there is a straighter path beyond the hills, the valleys, the curves, the mountains, and the detours. Trust God and choose your "Hard". Life is hard, no matter the direction you go, but know that some directions are harder than others. I would rather choose the "Hard" that would allow me to experience the highs of emotions: Joy, peace, freedom, and abundance, versus the "Hard" that would give me the lows of emotions: shame, guilt, fear, doubt, pressure, and lack. It is an honor and a privilege to be your mother, grandmother, and family. I love you all with all my heart.

To my new family, my readers, I want you to know that this book is meant to be a companion for you along this journey. You are not alone. I pray for your clarity and strength through this journey and that you will achieve your dreams and destiny.

ASCEND

from Paycheck to Prosperity

The Journey from Financial Stress and Struggle to Financial Freedom and Abundance

Table of Contents

Introduction
From Silent Struggle to Financial Strength

Jeremiah 29:11 (NIV) For I know the plans I have for you, declares the Lord, plans to prosper you and not to harm you, plans to give you hope and a future.

I've always dreamed of living a life without lack. Even before I could fully articulate what financial security meant, I longed for a life where I didn't have to worry about money—where peace, joy, and stability were the norm, not the exception. As a little girl growing up in a small town, I didn't dream of fame for its spotlight—I dreamed of comfort. Of beauty. Of freedom.

I imagined fireplaces glowing and toy trains circling through a life of joy and abundance. I wanted to live in a world where I didn't have to wonder if we could afford it. Where is the answer to "Can I have this?" wasn't measured in scarcity.

I once stood on a stage at a local pageant, a tiny and bright-eyed 9-year-old, declaring without hesitation and with full sincerity, when asked what I wanted to be when I grew up; I said, "A movie star." But it wasn't the red carpets or flashing lights that I craved—it was the life I thought came with it: security, options, and freedom.

That moment was captured in the local newspaper, and some people in my small town laughed at me, in particular, this one woman who worked at the local corner store. In a town where dreams often stayed small, mine felt outrageous. They couldn't see what I saw. More importantly, they could not see outside of their immediate surroundings. They didn't understand that this little girl wasn't dreaming of fame—she was dreaming of financial freedom.

You see, my desire to become a movie star didn't come from a hunger to be a celebrity—it was birthed from the soap operas I watched every afternoon: *All My Children*, *The Young and the Restless*, *One Life to Live*, and *General Hospital*. Those shows gave me a glimpse outside the borders of my small town and into a world of possibility. I saw business owners, company executives, doctors, and lawyers. I saw strong, capable women making decisions, leaving legacies, and living in beautiful homes with roaring fireplaces. I saw what generational wealth could look like.

I saw abundance –and I wanted that not just for me, but for my family as well. And more than anything, from the eyes of a little 9-year-old, I saw a life where I could one day have my own bedroom—something I shared with my sister growing up—and a home with a gorgeous fireplace and a big Christmas Tree with a toy train circling around it. I saw where I could one day give back to my mother and family in a way that truly changed and impacted their lives. That image lived in my heart as the picture of abundance: warmth, space, and something of my own.

But I didn't let go of that dream. Even then,

something in me believed that I was created for more. That little girl grew up. And while I didn't become a movie star, I did become a woman who pursued her dreams and created a life beyond what my environment predicted. A life where money no longer controlled me, but where I learned to manage it, respect it, and use it to build the life I once imagined from a child's heart.

And for a while, I looked like I had it all together. But behind the success, I carried the weight of financial stress that no one saw. I smiled through the struggle, performed through the pressure, and tried to outwork my overwhelm. Money had always been part of my story, but it wasn't until I faced the silence, shame, and systems that kept me stuck that I began to rise. This book is the roadmap I wish someone had handed me back when I was that little girl with the fireplace dream, and again as a grown woman silently drowning under the pressure to hold it all together. If you've ever dreamed of more, and not just wealth, but peace, this journey is for you. Because you, too, were never meant to just survive. You were meant to ascend.

My Money Story: The Rise Before the Rise

I never thought I'd be here — writing a book about financial empowerment. You see, I was going to open up multiple dental practices and manage them when I decided to leave the dental chair.

Life was going well, at least, from the outside looking in. I had accomplished many of the things I dreamed about as a little girl. I was a doctor. I owned a business. I had achieved success, opened not just one, but three dental practices, and was living the dream I had once imagined through the lens of soap operas and youthful longing.

For years, I was the one people came to for answers. I was a professional. The leader. The woman who "had it together."

Yes, I was making money — but I wasn't in control of it.

I didn't have a system. I didn't have a clear view of my expenses. I couldn't even tell you what was due when. I was running a business from a blind spot — shifting funds, juggling bills, hoping it would all somehow work itself out.

Behind the scenes, I was silently struggling. And every night, I went home carrying the shame, the stress, and the silent pressure of pretending I had it all together. I'd wake up at 4 a.m. with my chest tight, heart racing, trying to figure out how to stretch what I had just to meet what I owed.

Many times, with success comes an unimaginable level of weight. At least in my case, that was a reality. And somewhere along the way, that weight started crushing me. When I opened my third practice, things changed. What was once a well-oiled machine began to unravel. Turnover became my new reality-something I hadn't faced before. Employees left faster than I could hire replacements. I felt like I was putting out fires every day. The joy I once felt in my work started slipping away, replaced by stress, doubt, and fatigue. That third practice, though birthed with ambition, became a source of strain.

I eventually made the hard decision to close it. But closing the doors didn't close the debt. The weight of that financial obligation remained, and I transferred it to my original practice, the one that had always been my strongest. That decision unintentionally weakened my foundation. What was once my thriving, high-performing practice was now burdened under the strain of keeping everything afloat. And that's when the real financial battle began. The stress crept in slowly. At first-- late nights, anxious mornings, a tightness in my chest that wouldn't go away.

For a while, I looked like I had it all together. But behind the scenes, I carried the weight of financial stress that no one saw. I smiled through the struggle, performed through the pressure, and tried to outwork my overwhelm. Money had always been part of my story—but it wasn't until I faced the strain, silence, shame, and systems that kept me stuck that I began to rise.

I thought about filing for bankruptcy. In fact, I had three attorneys telling me to file for bankruptcy. I actually considered it seriously. But deep in my spirit, I kept hearing that still, small voice: "This is not your way out. There has to be another way," And there was.

I didn't take the route that others advised. I listened to what I knew was divine wisdom, even when it didn't make logical sense. I chose the path that would have me fight my way back. Not just erase it. It's the very path that I took that led to this book — and to the **ASCEND**

Coaching Program and Framework.

Not in a moment of glory, but in a valley of grit. It was in my struggle that I finally began to embrace the journey, not just the highs, but the healing, the learning, the rebuilding. I began to piece my finances back together, root by root, decision by decision. It wasn't easy. I cried. I doubted. I prayed. But I kept the faith and kept moving. And slowly but surely, I rebuilt not just my finances, but myself. I laid a new foundation-this time, one built on clarity, alignment, stewardship, and strategy.

This is more than a story of bounce-back. It's a testimony of what happens when you choose to believe in your future more than your fears. My journey through financial hardship taught me how to coach others through theirs. That's why I'm here. That's why you're reading this. Because now it's your turn to rise.

Money has always been a part of my story—not just the dollars and cents, but the emotions, the aspirations, and the silent battles that came with it. From wishing for a room of my own and toy trains circling around Christmas trees to navigating the realities of student loans, business ownership, and financial stress, my journey has been shaped by both lack and abundance. And through it all, I've discovered that financial freedom isn't just about what's in your bank account; it's about what you believe is possible for your life.

This book is the roadmap I wish someone had handed me—back when I was that little girl with the fireplace dream, and again as a grown woman silently drowning under the pressure to have it all together.

If you've ever dreamed of more—not just wealth, but peace—this journey is for you. Because you, too, were never meant to just survive. You were meant to ASCEND.

This book is not about budgeting tips or quick-fix hacks. It is about alignment. It is about controlling your financial narrative. It is about redefining and nurturing your new relationship with money. Ultimately, this book is about reclaiming your power.

This book takes you on a journey where you can drop shame and stress off along the way to arriving at clarity, confidence, and control. But most importantly, it is about aligning with who you were meant to become—even in the face of financial adversity.

What You'll Experience

As a Certified Financial Education Instructor, successful business owner, and a woman who once silently battled financial overwhelm behind a polished professional image, I don't just teach and speak about this—I've lived it. And I'm here to walk with you through the same transformation I experienced.

The book takes you on a journey through the ASCEND Framework, which is built on 6 Pillars of Strength and Strategy and encompasses a step-by-step path from paycheck to prosperity – designed for women who are ready to rise.

Each chapter guides you through a new pillar of the journey:

- ◊ **A – Awaken and Align Your Mindset: Honesty with your financial truth and beliefs**
- ◊ **S – Stabilize and Strengthen Your Financial Foundation: Goals, Values, & Financial Focus**
- ◊ **C – Control and Clarify Your Cash Flow and Financial Narrative**
- ◊ **E – Eliminate and Elevate Above What's Been Holding You Down: Mindset, Money, Purpose, Debt Reduction**
- ◊ **N – Nurture and Navigate Towards Your Future: Credit Score, Networth, Savings, Banking**
- ◊ **D – Design and Dominate Your Prosperity Plan: Building your 7-Figure Bank Account; and Seeing the Plan in full and how it has worked in real-life transformations; Built on wealth, peace, and purpose**

Whether you're an executive, entrepreneur, team leader, or a woman holding it all together behind the scenes…

If you've ever looked successful on the outside, but struggled silently on the inside and behind closed doors… this is your space.
If you've ever earned good money but felt like you had nothing to show for it… this book is for you.
If you're ready to finally align your success with financial strength, confidence, and power… you're in the right place.

If you want a new story, a new money narrative, this is your season.

You are not behind. And you are not alone. Your story doesn't end in survival.

You are "ASCENDing" now.

ASCEND is the bridge between survival and stewardship — from confusion to confidence, from financial strain to overflow. It is not just a financial guide, but it is a transformational roadmap.

By the end of the book, you will:

- Shift from paycheck to paycheck to powerfully planning your money
- Establish systems for saving, debt reduction, and net worth growth
- Gain peace of mind and stop fearing your finances
- Build a path toward consistent positive cash flow and a **6-figure** bank account
- Activate **financial freedom** and begin walking in **abundance**

TRANSITION FROM INTRODUCTION TO CHAPTER 1

You've made it here — not by accident, but by alignment.

Maybe your heart is still racing from the pressures of financial stress, yet you are still moving daily with the rigors of a career. Maybe you are like so many other women who are working hard but still feeling financially behind, putting in the effort but not seeing the fruit of your labor. Maybe you're carrying silent shame, or waking up at 4 a.m. like I once did, wondering how you're going to make it all work. And the hardest part of all this is that you feel you know better and should not be in this position: a position of confusion and lack.

But you know what? You showed up anyway. And that matters more than you know.

Before we talk about numbers, we're going to talk about *narratives* — the ones we inherited, the ones we absorbed, and the ones we've silently lived by for far too long.

Financial narratives that speak for us influence our decisions and our actions. Narratives that handicap us, hold us down, and paralyze our thought process.

Because real change starts in your mind.

This part of your financial journey is where your shift begins — not with spreadsheets, but with truth. With healing. With awakening. Because real change starts in your mind.

Let's take the first step of the ASCEND journey together.

Transformation Spotlights and Interludes

Throughout this book, you'll meet some courageous women whose transformations began when they chose to rewrite their money stories. Each woman's story is a window into a different path of financial transformation, from single motherhood to business growth, from burnout to breakthrough. Their stories are both personal and universal, and they reflect the power of clarity, coaching, faith, and financial strategy. These are some of my clients with whom I have worked with. The names and occupations have been changed for confidentiality purposes.

Let their stories inspire your next step.

Reflection Questions:

1. Which woman's story resonated with you most, and why?

2. What similarities do you see in your journey and theirs?

3. What transformation are you believing in your own life?

Where Are You in Your Financial Journey?

Take a moment to answer these five questions honestly — no shame, no guilt. Just truth. This is your snapshot.

For each question, answer Yes or No.

1. Do you know how much income you bring in each month (after taxes)?

2. Do you know how much you spend each month — and where it goes?

3. Do you know how much total debt you have and what interest rate(s) you're paying?

4. Do you know your net worth — and do you track it at least once a year?

5. Do you have dreams or goals that require funding — but you don't yet know how much they cost or where to start financially?

How to Score Yourself

Give yourself 1 point for every "Yes" you confidently answered.

- 0–1 points → Surviving
  You're carrying invisible stress and may be reacting month to month without full clarity. You're not alone — this is where many women begin.

- 2–3 points → Stabilizing
  You're starting to gain awareness, but may still feel unsure or scattered. The foundations are forming — keep going.

- 4 points → Growing
  You have some key pieces in place and are moving forward with intention. With deeper systems, you'll gain even more momentum.

- 5 points → Thriving
  You have clarity, control, and a vision. Now it's about expanding, refining, and walking in overflow with purpose.

Use this as a compass, not a judgment. Your score is not your identity; it's simply a compass. It tells you where you are, not where you'll stay. The chapters ahead will guide you from surviving to thriving; step by step, with clarity, faith, and strategy.

Chapter 1
Awaken and Align Your Mindset

"Do not conform to the pattern of this world but be transformed by the renewing of your mind." — Romans 12:2

I remember the moment I realized that the way I thought about money had been quietly shaping my life for years. I was sitting in my office, juggling my dental practices, wondering why I felt financially overwhelmed. I had success by every outward measure—but behind the scenes, my thoughts were filled with anxiety, fear, confusion, and silent shame. The stress wasn't just in my bank account. It was in my mind.

Maybe you've been there too—working hard, showing up strong, but quietly battling I'll never pay off my debt or experience financial freedom thoughts like, "I'll never get ahead," "I'm bad with money," or "This is just the way it is." These are the *silent beliefs* that wage *loud battles* against your peace. And they don't just sit in the background—they drive your decisions, influence your habits, and limit your vision for what's possible.

What if it's not just your income that needs to shift—but your internal narrative?
What if your breakthrough begins not with more money, but with a renewed mindset?

So, let's pull into the first rest area of the journey. Here, we'll explore how your thoughts, upbringing, and inner money stories may be holding you back—and how awakening to the truth can begin your journey toward freedom. You'll learn how to identify false beliefs, rewrite your financial narrative, and align your mind with the abundance, peace, and prosperity God has already set aside for you.

Why Mindset Matters More Than Math

"Before you change your money, you must change your mind."

Contrary to what many believe, financial peace doesn't start with a bigger check or more money. Many of us believe that if I could just take on an extra shift or bring in a little more money an hour, that all my money ailments will somehow disappear. It sounds good. But bringing in more money in a broken cash flow system with leaking holes only allows for more money to leak out, with you still not knowing where it went. Financial peace starts with alignment. Aligning your money with your values and priorities. It starts with truth; your truth about your money mindset.

What Is a Money Mindset?

Your **money mindset** is the collection of beliefs, habits, and emotional patterns you carry around money. It's shaped by what you saw growing up with your parents and family, what you heard from friends or colleagues, or how you experienced lack, just enough, or abundance.

Many of us never question it. We just repeat what we saw or experienced — often in silence, shame, and guilt. My financial breakthrough began at my "4AM awaken call". I now believe it was God calling me to a place higher in my mind and my finances. I just couldn't see it at first. I was so weighed down by the pressure of the Silent, secret financial burden I carried.

I know that many of you reading this book are experiencing this same denial. But I believe that if you are reading this book, God is calling you to a higher place as well. This book and chapter are about you confronting your silence. It's about awakening your awareness, rewriting your financial narrative, and reclaiming your power.

Financial breakthrough starts in the mind. Before the numbers changed, the narrative in my mind had to change. That's why this chapter opens with a bold truth: mindset matters more than math, and the first step in the ASCEND process is Awakening.

Your money beliefs—formed from childhood, culture, and past financial failures or experiences—shape every financial decision you make. If you believe you'll always struggle, you'll unconsciously sabotage your success. If you believe you're not 'good with money,' you'll avoid responsibility. That's not a flaw—it's conditioning.

I invite you to pause and evaluate your current mindset, not from a place of blame, but with compassion and curiosity. Ask yourself: What do I believe about money? About success? About myself? Your answers will reveal the roots of your current reality.

Changing your narrative doesn't mean ignoring your circumstances—it means confronting them with a new lens. As you learn to reframe failure, challenge lies, and affirm new truths, you'll begin to see that your greatest financial shift will always begin with your thoughts.

Silent Beliefs, Loud Battles

I've sat in rooms with powerful, brilliant women — nurse practitioners, lawyers, business owners, ministry leaders, working moms, and many other career women — all secretly battling the same enemy: a broken money mindset and cash flow system.

Not because they weren't smart. Not because they weren't capable. Not even because they were not making the money. But because somewhere along the way, they inherited a financial belief system that was limiting, stressful, and misaligned with their truth and values.

And for a long time… so did I. I believed I had to figure everything out alone. I believed asking for help made me weak. I believed I could outwork the problem of a broken cash flow system — all I needed was a few more hours in the day. I would work from sunup to sundown. I believed my hustle would heal my broken cash flow. But I realized that hustle was not the medicine; clarity was what actually eased my pain.

We all carry silent beliefs-internal narratives whispered by our past, culture, or experiences. These beliefs often speak louder than facts and shape our relationship with money long before we ever earn our first paycheck. These internal scripts, though silent, fuel loud external battles. When we don't address our silent beliefs, we find ourselves repeating self-sabotaging patterns that hinder our progress and keep us bound.

To win the battle externally, we must first identify and challenge the lies we've silently accepted as truth.

Reflection Questions:

1. What early messages shaped how you view money today?

2. What internal battles are you fighting silently when it comes to finances?

3. What belief do you need to rewrite to move forward with peace and power?

The Silence Behind the Success

Why do women stay stuck silently? It's our shame and guilt, fear of judgment, and for many women, especially professionals, leaders, and business owners, there's an unspoken pressure to "*have it all together*". On the outside, you're the one others admire and look up to and respect for your accomplishments. But on the inside, you might be silently:

- Juggling bills while managing a business
- Feeling embarrassed about debt or disorganization
- Avoiding your bank statements or credit reports

because of negative balances or lower scores

- Wondering how you got here when you "should've known better"

I would wake up early every morning with the struggle of how to go into my office and lead my team. How could I lead them when I didn't have direction in my life? How could I guide them when I had lost my compass? All the questions I asked myself. But each morning, I would pull myself out of the bedroom, the place I had retreated to because it gave me the isolation I longed for inside the four walls and held my secret. But in reality, it kept me bound and stuck and clothed in silent shame and guilt.

"I lived with the shame of knowing I should have been further along and the guilt and fear of admitting that something wasn't working... I lived with the fear of it all falling apart and the stress and strain from navigating from a place of confusion and not knowing.

This silence becomes a heavy burden — because it isolates you, keeps you in a box, and keeps the weights around your ankles. Your thoughts torment you. Tell you that you are stupid for where you are for the decisions you made, the moves you made, and the money you spent. And the biggest lie is that you are the only one in this situation or dealing with these circumstances. But you must remember that all have fallen in one way or another. The key is not to stay down and to remove yourself from isolation. Surround yourself with other women changing their lives, reclaiming their power, and rewriting their money story. Join our community!

Women ASCENDing Group

The Weight of Financial Shame and Guilt

You see, shame said to me, *"There's something wrong with me."* And guilt says, *"I did something wrong."* Both of these are powerful emotional weights that can lead to your inaction and avoidance, secret financial struggles, reluctance to ask for help, and a cycle of self-sabotage.

"Every night, I went home carrying the shame, the stress, and the silent pressure of pretending I had it all together. I would do this day after day, night after night, waking up early in the morning consistently at 4AM, until the weight was unsustainable. I came to a breaking point one morning. I had no idea how to pull myself from under the pressure. I was at my lowest. I got out of my bed and I told God I was standing on his word. At that moment, I literally put the Bible on the floor and I stood on it. I continued to tell God that I was standing on his word. It was then that I began to embrace my journey. I was committed to owning my story, rewriting my money narrative, and reclaiming my power.

Lies We Tell Ourselves About Money

Have you ever found yourself saying, 'I'm not good with money,' or 'I'm broke,' or 'I'll always be in debt'? These statements, though often said casually, are powerful affirmations that shape how we view ourselves…

These are lies we tell ourselves–not because we want to be dishonest, but because somewhere along the way, those lies felt like safety or reality…

By confronting these lies, we create space for truth…

The path to prosperity requires us to uproot falsehoods and replace them with faith, strategy, and self-awareness.

Many of our deepest money beliefs were never chosen; they were inherited. From what we heard growing up, to what we observed in our homes or in the media, churches, schools, and communities, these messages became our financial script. And often, that script is outdated and disempowering. The messages you carry are oftentimes not conscious to you, but they limit your ability to grow, succeed, or take necessary action. These limiting money messages unknowingly surround your finances.

It is imperative to identify them, understand their origin and their impact on your finances and reframe them in such a way that they no longer hinder your progress but support your progression along your financial journey.

You may have heard things like, "Money doesn't grow on trees, We can't afford that, and Rich people are greedy." You may find yourself developing some of your own, for example, "I'm just not good with money. I'll always be in debt. People like me don't become wealthy. If I make more money, I'll lose it anyway. Or, I could never be financially free."

You may have seen fear-based decisions being made or interfering with decisions needing to be made, silence around finances, or even shame or ridicule attached to desire. These subtle cues become powerful internal narratives that feed your financial script.

Blaming your past is not productive, but what will move you along this journey is recognizing that you've absorbed them, so you can decide what to keep and what to release.

You are not obligated to carry beliefs or lies that no longer serve your future. But you must first identify them before you can let them go. When you become aware of your inherited money messages, you take back your power. You begin to write a new financial script—one rooted in truth, abundance, stewardship, and alignment. That's where lasting transformation begins—not just in your budget, but in your beliefs and thoughts.

To allow an unhealthy financial script to continue will cause you to repeat self-sabotaging financial patterns, not take financial action (debt reduction, saving, budgeting), or even undervalue your work and worth.

Reflection Questions:

1. What lie about money have you believed most often?

2. Where did that belief come from; and is it still serving you?

3. What truth do you want to replace that lie with?

Silencing the Shame and Shifting the Story: The D.R.E.A.M. Mindset Makeover

For many women, financial stress isn't just about numbers — it's about narratives.

It's the quiet shame of feeling like you should be further along.
It's the hidden guilt of success on the outside, but chaos behind the curtain.
It's the internal war between what you desire and what you believe you deserve.

Guilt. Shame. And Silence. These are the invisible weights many of us carry — and they often stem from beliefs we never chose but simply inherited. Before we ever miss a payment or overspend on a card, we often carry unspoken beliefs that shape how we see money, how we handle it, and how we see *ourselves*.

But here's the truth: You are not your past decisions. You are not the dollar amount in your account, positive or negative amounts. You are not a financial failure. You are capable. You are worthy. You are called to more.

That's why the journey to financial transformation must begin in the mind — because you can't build freedom on top of guilt, abundance on top of silence, or prosperity on top of shame. You must shift your beliefs before you shift your bank account.

Releasing the Silence: A Shift Begins with Truth

The moment we speak the truth is the moment shame begins to lose its grip and guilt dims its light. Here's the truth you need to hear. A broken cash flow system is not a moral failure. It is a financial circumstance — and you are not stuck there. You are not irresponsible. You are not behind. You're just in a transformation phase. And that deserves grace, not guilt.

I witnessed and experienced this by moving from silence into strategy. That turning point became the birth of ASCEND — not just as my framework, but as a movement of healing and power in my life. I am writing this book because I want you to experience your healing, freedom, and peace.

To every woman reading this book, you are not your balance. You are not your bank account. You are not the overdraft, the debt, or the delinquency. You are a woman of wisdom. And today, shame and guilt are no more. They must go. You don't need more status quo and perfection. It's time to give yourself permission to begin again. This is your season where your mindset shifts and your money follows. You are no longer surviving. You are ASCENDing!

So, I am asking you to walk through your journey one step at a time. It's important for you to define the beliefs that you are carrying, release them as they are lies that are holding you back from your destiny of financial freedom and prosperity. Affirm your new truth and new money narrative and move with clarity and intention.

And that's where the **D.R.E.A.M. Mindset Makeover** comes in — your pathway out of guilt, shame, silence, and your limiting money messages into clarity, confidence, and freedom.

The D.R.E.A.M. Mindset Makeover

"A Mindset Shift for Your Money Story"

Let's walk it out:

D – Define the Beliefs You Carry

What do you *really* believe about money? About financial freedom? About yourself? What did you see, hear, or experience growing up? Write it down. Don't filter it. It starts with honesty. Maybe you've silently repeated,
"I'm just not good with my money," or
"I make it, but I can't keep it. I'll always be broke." or
"I should be further along by now." or

"I can never save my money because something always happens and takes it away."

These are not facts. They are beliefs and your

untruths about your money. And beliefs can be changed. Until you define them, they'll quietly drive your decisions and your spending habits. So, take inventory. Name the thought patterns. Bring them to the light. Because what remains unspoken stays unhealed.

R – Release the Guilt, Shame, and Lies

Now that you've defined the lies and beliefs that you are carrying, ask: Is this serving me and my future? Many of our beliefs were never ours to begin with — they were passed down through generations, trauma, culture, experiences, or fear. Some were born from moments of lack or not enough. Others from experiences of what we saw as a failure. Maybe you lost a business, didn't pay your car or credit card on time, or spent too much on vacation. Whatever your experiences are, it's time to let go. This is your permission slip to release what was never meant to stay. You are allowed to grow beyond the beliefs that kept you surviving. You're allowed to evolve. You don't have to fear your own success.

You don't have to repeat financial dysfunction just because it's familiar.

E – Envision the Possibility

What would your life look like if money weren't a source of stress? Who could you become if money were no longer a source of fear? So, I want you to close your eyes and imagine paying your bills without panic or pressure, having savings that you could count on and not return to the next week to withdraw from, or building wealth from a place of clarity and confidence. I want you to imagine your world waking up with calmness and not financial panic, paying your bills a month ahead of the due date, or having savings with 6 months of income for just your monthly expenses.

Envisioning is not daydreaming — it's direction-setting. You can't pursue what you can't picture. So, give yourself permission to imagine what's possible. You can't pursue what you can't picture.

A – Affirm Your New Truth

This is where shame gets silenced and truth gets activated. So, speak what's true, even if it's not fully visible yet.

Speak life into your new beliefs. Speak them even when you don't feel them yet.
"I am a wise steward."
"I manage my money with clarity and intention."
"I attract opportunities aligned with my purpose."

"I will never have a negative cash flow system ever again because money flows to me continuously with purpose and alignment."

Affirmations aren't fluff — they're fuel along the journey. They give you focus.
Your words frame your world, so choose truth over fear. Your words are seeds for your new financial narrative. Plant them wisely.

M – Move with Clarity and Intention

Now that your thoughts are aligned, what action can you take? Awareness without action keeps you parked in the same space. It's time to take the next step. Small steps create big shifts — but only if you move. This might be the week that you

- Finally, looking at your expenses and tracking them for the first time
- Creating Your Financial Freedom Spending Plan
- Saying "no" to things that drain you or are not aligned with your money values
- Saying "yes" to the support, guidance, or accountability you need

You don't need a full blueprint to begin — just one brave, clear, intentional move in the direction of your freedom.

The Lesson My Mother Gave Me

One day, while treating a young patient who needed a cavity filled, his mother tried to console him by saying, "At least you don't have to go to school today." I smiled and asked, "Why not?" He wasn't sick or injured — and I knew skipping school for something small was a missed opportunity to build something far more important than comfort: work ethic.

I shared with her what my mother told me when I was a young girl:
"Baby, when your menstrual cycle starts, you're still going to school. You'll have it most of your life, so

there's no need to think you can stay home every month."

It might sound small, but it shaped me. I went to school, earned years of perfect attendance, and learned to push through discomfort and challenging situations in my life. Dental school challenged me like nothing before. That lesson stayed with me when dental school felt like a never-ending uphill climb. I had always been a strong academic student, but here, I was stretched, tested, and pushed to my limits. At the time, I didn't understand why God was allowing it. It wasn't until a year after graduation, walking down the hallway to my very first dental practice, that it hit me: "I get it now, God."

He had been preparing me to stand with broad shoulders and a firm stance in a profession dominated by men — ready to handle the challenges from patients, contractors, and peers. That resilience is the same quality I draw on to face financial challenges and keep moving forward.

My mother's voice still echoes in my mind: *"Baby, you're still going to school."* She wasn't just talking about attendance — she was teaching me perseverance. That work ethic became the backbone of my life. It carried me through dental school when I felt like quitting, through the uncertainty of business ownership, and through the weight of my heaviest financial seasons.

That same grit is what allowed me to face my numbers honestly, build a plan, and stick to it when it would have been easier to walk away. It's why I believe you can rise from wherever you are right now.

A Purpose Bigger Than You: What Is Your Why?

Every woman has a deeper reason for wanting financial change, but many have never taken the time to name it. Naming it allows you to identify your why. Your 'why' is not just a goal—it's your anchor when the journey gets hard. It's the heartbeat behind your budget, your sacrifice, and your vision. It's the light to your path.

Maybe your "why" is your children. Maybe it's breaking a generational pattern of poverty and lack. Maybe it's living a life of generosity or building something bigger than you. Whatever it is, when your 'why' is clear, your decisions become clearer, and your actions line up with your desires. It gives meaning and purpose to every dollar saved, every debt paid off, and every deposit made towards your net worth.

Too often, women think they're bad with money when in reality, they've just never been connected to a reason bigger than just getting up, going to work, and paying their bills. This section is about finding that reason. Because when your money is connected to mission, you move differently—you move with intention, deliberateness, and power.

Start by asking: What future am I building? Who benefits when I win? What legacy do I want to have? Your 'why' doesn't have to be fancy—but it must be real. And when it is, it will pull you forward even on the hardest financial days, when there is no money left from the paycheck, when things break down and need repairs. Your 'why' cannot be someone else's. Your "why" is unique to you. It can't be borrowed or copied.

Your "why" should be something so important to you that thinking or talking about it makes you emotional. It needs to light a fire under you, and it should be something you don't want to live without. Your "why" should remind you every step of the journey that giving up is no longer an option. It may be helpful for you to create a picture of it and place it in a place that you see every day as motivation to keep you pushing forward and motivating you along the way.

Access Bonus Material from Dr. Juanita

Owning Your Money Story

Every woman has a money story—even if she's never spoken it out loud. It's the internal script shaped by experiences, family dynamics, financial wins, and painful lessons. It's the story behind how we spend, save, earn, or avoid money altogether. But here's the truth: that story is not set in stone. It can be edited, challenged, and rewritten. And for many of us, it must be—because the version we've been living no longer serves the life we're trying to build. It's time to stop hiding your story and start owning it.

For years, I was silently navigating two worlds: the public image of a successful dentist and businesswoman… and the private weight of financial stress and hidden obligations. My practice was thriving on paper, but behind the scenes, I was juggling cash flow issues, unexpected expenses, and the quiet fear that everything could crumble with one unexpected event. When the pandemic hit, that fear wasn't hypothetical anymore—it became my reality. My office shut down, revenue halted, and I had to make decisions that felt like survival, not strategy.

But that experience, while painful, forced me to confront my money story. I had to look at the patterns I had been repeating—overworking, under-saving, saying yes to others while saying no to my own financial security. I realized I had been carrying beliefs that success had to come with stress, that taking care of others financially meant putting myself last, and that abundance was something I had to hustle for constantly. I had been writing a story of burnout masked as achievement.

That's when I chose to rewrite my money narrative. I restructured my finances, revisited every belief I held about money, and began building a life and legacy rooted in peace, purpose, and prosperity. I didn't just want to survive—I wanted to ASCEND. And I knew that if I could transform my financial life from the inside out, other women could too. That's why this program, this book, and this journey were born—not just from strategy, but from my story. Because financial transformation doesn't start with numbers, it starts with the narrative.

“When I stopped hiding behind the image of success, I finally started building a life of peace, purpose, and prosperity. Owning your story means reclaiming the power you once gave away. It means looking at where you’ve been without shame, so you can decide where you’re going with purpose and intention.

Reflection Questions:

1. How would you describe your money story up until now?

2. What emotions come up when you think about your financial past?

3. What part of your story are you ready to take ownership of and rewrite?

Dr. Juanita’s Word of Truth

“From Shame to Strength”

Here’s what I want you to know: Shame is not your truth. Debt is not your identity.
And guilt is not your guide. If you’ve been carrying financial guilt — for past mistakes, poor decisions, or just not knowing what you didn’t know — it’s time to lay it down.

Because here’s the truth: **You don’t need more money to be free — you need more clarity, courage,**

and alignment.

Let me say that again for the woman in the back row of her life: You don't need more hustle. You need healing. You need a strategy. You need space to breathe and begin again.

My story proves that you don't need more money. I just needed to be better with the money that I made. Releasing shame and guilt was the first step toward my financial freedom — but it wasn't the only one. I also had to recognize the quiet strength that had been with me all along.

Shame can keep you stuck, but grit will keep you moving. And when you combine the freedom of releasing guilt with the discipline of showing up, you unlock a power that no setback can take away. You are not defined by what you've been through — you are defined by what you *press through.*

Shame thrives in silence. But your story is shifting now. You're not just dreaming about a better financial future — you're *defining* it, *releasing* what no longer fits, *envisioning* what's possible, *affirming* what's true, and *moving* toward it like the powerful, purpose-driven woman you are.

You are no longer bound by lies. You are breaking cycles. You are rewriting your money story — with clarity, with courage, and with faith. This is your season of awakening. As you realign your thoughts, your financial reality will begin to mirror your renewed mindset. Keep speaking life, keep uprooting the lies, keep planting seeds of truth, and keep "D.R.E.A.M.ing".

Your new chapter begins now. Welcome to the D.R.E.A.M. shift. Welcome to your financial freedom mindset.

Your Affirmation:

"I release the lies I once believed about money and embrace the truth of who I am: a wise, worthy, and powerful steward. My mind is renewed, my vision is clear, and I move with intention toward prosperity and peace. I am no longer bound by shame and fear — I am aligned, awakened, and ASCENDing."

Chapter 2

Stabilize and Strengthen Your Finances

"By wisdom a house is built, and through understanding it is established; through knowledge its rooms are filled with rare and beautiful treasures." — Proverbs 24:3–4

Stability doesn't happen by accident — it's created by intention. Strength isn't just about what you earn; it's about what you protect, preserve, and prepare for the future. You can have a good income and still live on shaky ground if your money is unmanaged and unprotected. But when you decide to stabilize, you shift from being reactive to being proactive. And when you strengthen, you make sure the progress you've worked so hard for isn't easily undone.

There was a time in my life when everything looked solid from the outside, but inside, I knew I was one unexpected bill away from a breakdown. I was living at the corner of *Financial Struggle Freeway* and *Silent Shame Boulevard*. My income was steady, but my peace was shaky. I thought I was being responsible with money — after all, I wasn't a big shopper — but I was unprepared. I didn't have a system. I had a cycle.

Every month, I spent without first considering my production for that month, whether income was up or down. I made large purchases I believed were wise — equipment for my dental practice, assets I thought would increase my net worth — but they weren't part of a plan. They were unbudgeted, unstrategized, and unaligned with a bigger picture. And while my intentions were good, the lack of structure left me stuck: low on cash flow, weighted down, and unprepared for the unexpected.

More importantly, my decisions and finances weren't rooted in the ultimate building blocks — the Word of God. Without that foundation, my financial house was missing its most vital support beams. Scripture teaches us to build on wisdom, stewardship, trust, gratitude, and generosity. The Bible is full of principles for financial management, but they have to move from head knowledge to heart truth. The psalmist writes, *"I have hidden your word in my heart, that I might not sin against you"* (Psalm 119:11). When the Word becomes your blueprint, you can bend, pivot, and adjust without breaking. Your thoughts, actions, and decisions come into alignment with God's design — leading you into stability, abundance, and prosperity.

The Bible tells us, *"By wisdom a house is built, and through understanding it is established; through knowledge its rooms are filled with rare and beautiful treasures"* (Proverbs 24:3–4). I began to picture my finances as a house. The foundation wasn't just concrete — it was the Word of God.

In this house, every wall represented a principle from scripture:

- **Stewardship**: Faithfully managing what God has placed in your hands (Luke 16:10).

- **Trust**: Believing God is your source, not your paycheck (Philippians 4:19).
- **Gratitude**: Recognizing and thanking Him for His provision (1 Thessalonians 5:18).
- **Generosity**: Giving as an act of worship and obedience (Proverbs 11:25).

The roof was *protection* — God's covering over my finances when I honored His principles. Inside the house were the "rooms" of my financial life: savings, giving, investments, debt management, and daily expenses. Each room needed order, just as Proverbs says they should be "filled with rare and beautiful treasures."

This is why I want to share with you the story, *The House That Wisdom Built*. Scripture comes alive when we see it in story form — it moves from being a set of verses to becoming a lived experience. Just like a home needs a strong foundation, your finances need to be anchored in truth. When your systems are built on God's wisdom, your financial structure can weather storms without collapsing.

The House That Wisdom Built

A Financial Parable Based on God's Principles

There was once a woman who had dreams larger than her income, a heart that loved deeply, and hands that worked tirelessly. She lived in a modest home, but her vision was grand — not for status, but for stability. She longed to create a life of peace, purpose, and provision.

At first, she built without a plan. Her days were full of hustle, her nights full of worry. She made money, but the money made no peace. She gave generously but never saved. She spent money quickly but never tracked it. Her home looked fine from the outside, but cracks began to form in the foundation.

One night, in the quiet of her room, she whispered, "Lord, there must be more than this. I want to be free. I want to build something that lasts."

And a gentle truth stirred in her soul. And He whispered back through wisdom.

"Every strong house begins with wisdom. And wisdom starts with clarity."

So she began again — not by working more, but by seeing more. She laid down a new blueprint: Heaven's blueprint.

She started with the **foundation of stewardship**, remembering that everything she had was not really hers — she was simply managing what already belonged to God. *"The earth is the Lord's, and everything in it."* So, she began to treat her finances not just as currency, but as a calling.

She learned that *what she did with little mattered greatly*. So, she began to track even the smallest amounts. She paid attention. She wrote things down. She honored her inflow and guarded her outflow. Because she now believed: *"If I am faithful with little, I will be trusted with more."*

She made a choice to live below her means, not because she lacked — but because she was finally living with wisdom. She stopped wasting what she once called “extra” and started saving it. A small jar by the window held coins at first… then bills… then peace. She remembered what the wise had said: *“The wise store up, but the foolish spend everything they have.”*

Debt no longer defined her. She began paying what she owed, not just to clear the balances, but to walk in integrity. She stopped living as the borrower and started becoming the lender — not just financially, but emotionally and spiritually. She chose freedom over façade. *“The borrower is slave to the lender,”* she whispered, as she cut up a credit card with trembling hands and a steady heart.

She gave again — but this time, not out of guilt or pressure, but with expectation. Because she now believed in the promise: *“Give, and it will be given to you... a good measure, pressed down, shaken together, and running over.”* She smiled each time she gave, knowing that heaven’s economy was never empty.

And when doubt crept in, she remembered the words of the ancient prophets:

“Test Me in this... and see if I will not throw open the windows of heaven and pour out a blessing you can’t contain.”

Soon, the house began to change. The roof didn’t leak fear anymore. The walls echoed peace instead of pressure. And her floors — once unstable with worry — were now solid with wisdom.

Her finances didn't change overnight, but her focus did. And because her focus changed, her fruit did too. She was no longer the woman hoping to survive — she became the woman planning to prosper. As her wealth grew, she didn't boast. She remembered this, too:

"It is the blessing of the Lord that brings wealth, and He adds no sorrow with it."

She began to lend to others — not just money, but wisdom. She shared her story, not from a stage, but around kitchen tables and coffee shops, telling other women, "You don't need more stuff. You need more truth."

And as she stood at the door of her house — not large but filled with laughter — she looked around and saw abundance: a life no longer leaking, a plan no longer patched, and a soul no longer striving. This was the house that wisdom built. And it stood firm, not because of what she had, but because of what she *honored.*

And when others came to visit, they didn't just see a house — they saw a sanctuary. Not because it was perfect. But because it was built on purpose with Heaven's Blueprint.

Reflected Scriptures (woven into the story)

- **Luke 6:38** – *"Give, and it will be given to you..."*
- **Malachi 3:10** – *"Test Me in this... I will pour out a blessing..."*

- **Matthew 6:19–21** – *"Do not store up for yourselves treasures on earth..."*
- **Proverbs 10:22** – *"The blessing of the Lord brings wealth, without painful toil for it."*
- **Deuteronomy 15:6** – *"You will lend to many... and borrow from none."*
- **Proverbs 37:21** – (Interpreted as *living with integrity; paying what is owed*)
- **Proverbs 22:7** – *"The borrower is slave to the lender."*
- **Proverbs 21:20** – *"The wise store up... but fools gulp theirs down."*
- **Luke 16:10** – *"Whoever is faithful with little will be faithful with much."*
- **Psalm 24:1** – *"The earth is the Lord's, and everything in it."*

But here's what I learned: a house built without God's wisdom might look fine for a while, but storms will reveal the cracks. And my financial storms did just that. The blessing was that I could rebuild — but this time, I built with His Word as my blueprint.

Maybe you've lived at *Financial Struggle Freeway* or *Silent Shame Boulevard*. The money comes in, the bills go out, but there's no structure to support your goals. You "kind of" know your numbers, but when asked how much you make and how much you spend, your answers are vague guesses. Expenses creep higher without you realizing it — and in today's culture, early paycheck withdrawals have added a dangerous twist. What seems like a convenience often becomes a trap: smaller paychecks, more unplanned spending, and no full check left to cover major bills. Over time, this cycle shifts from survival into disaster — and disaster was never meant to be your permanent address.

In this chapter, we'll dismantle the patterns that keep you in financial instability. We'll build a system that supports your peace and strengthens your foundation. You'll learn how to eliminate the leaks that are weakening your financial house, and you'll discover strategies to reinforce and protect it — brick by brick, decision by decision, and dollar by dollar.

On a scale of 1-10, with 10 being financial relief efforts (consolidation or bankruptcy), what is your stress level? What would it feel like to have stability, not just income? What kind of strength could you walk in if your financial foundation were secure?

In this chapter, we're going to take the stress out of your finances by building a system that supports your peace. You'll learn how to eliminate the leaks that are cracking your foundation and drowning you. You will also learn some strategies to help enhance and support your financial structure that works for your life, and begin strengthening your financial base brick by brick, decision by decision, dollar by dollar.

Stabilizing Your Finances

Stability is the foundation on which all financial growth is built. You can have big dreams, lofty goals, and a vision board filled with inspiring images, but if your financial base is shaky, it's like building a house on sand. Stabilizing your finances means creating consistency — not just in income, but in management. It's about getting your feet planted firmly so you can move from crisis mode into confidence. Stability doesn't mean you'll never face challenges, but it does mean you'll be able to withstand them without crumbling.

For many women, financial life has felt like a constant balancing act — juggling bills, managing debt, and trying to save what's left over. But true stability begins when you stop reacting to your money and start leading it. It's when you shift from hoping "it all works out" to knowing you have a plan, a system, and a safety net. Strengthening your finances builds on that stability by fortifying the systems you've put in place, making them resilient enough to weather unexpected expenses, life transitions, or income changes.

When you stabilize and strengthen your finances, you give yourself more than numbers on a spreadsheet — you give yourself peace. You create the space to make intentional decisions instead of desperate ones. You free up mental energy to focus on growth, purpose, and legacy instead of being consumed by financial survival. Strength isn't just about earning more; it's about protecting, directing, and multiplying what you already have. This is where you move from fragile to fortified and from uncertainty to unshakable confidence.

Stabilizing your finances isn't just about plugging holes — it's about building on solid ground so you can create something that lasts. This is the phase where intention meets structure, where you shift from reacting to your money to leading it with purpose. You stop living in survival mode and start operating with direction, discipline, and alignment.

But before you can strengthen your foundation, you must identify what's weakening it. I call these *financial leaks* — the slow, often unnoticed drips that drain your resources and rob you of peace. Left unchecked, these leaks can quietly erode your progress, no matter how much money you make. Common examples include banking fees, impulse or unplanned purchases, check cashing services, early paycheck withdrawals, lack of an emergency fund, carrying too many credit cards, and more.

Your leaks may look different, but the impact is the same: money that could be building your future is slipping through the cracks. The goal in this phase is to spot those cracks, seal them with intentional action, and redirect those resources toward your goals.

When you start plugging leaks, your money begins to reflect your values instead of your stress. You begin asking the deeper questions: *What really matters to me? What am I building toward? Where is my money going — and is it carrying me closer to the life I want?*

Stabilizing means stepping out of blindness and into awareness. It's not about being perfect with money, but it is more about being purposeful, intentional, and deliberate.

Setting short-term goals becomes a tool for focus. Whether it's building a $500 emergency fund, making a debt snowball list, or finally tracking your spending, each small step becomes a brick in your foundation.

Stabilization teaches you that confidence grows with consistency. You don't need to do everything at once. You just need to keep moving in the direction of clarity.

This stage is also where your emotional relationship with money begins to heal. You start releasing shame, embracing your progress, and recognizing that every decision is a chance to honor your future. You don't have to apologize for wanting financial peace. And you don't need permission to go after it.

Stabilization is where you reclaim your voice. Most importantly, stabilizing is where vision and habits meet. You ground yourself in your "why," you align your actions with your priorities, and you build systems to support your new path. From this space, you begin to experience a steady rhythm. And with rhythm comes consistency and confidence. And with consistency and confidence, you finally begin to believe you can do this.

Reflection Questions

1. Where in your financial life do you feel the most unstable—and what would a solid foundation look like in that area?

2. What systems, habits, or small changes could help reinforce your base this month?

3. If your financial life were a building, what would the foundation need to hold everything you're dreaming of?

Strengthening Your Financial Base

Before you build anything lasting—whether it's wealth, a business, or a new beginning—you need a strong financial base. This phase is about securing your footing, organizing the essentials, and laying down the systems that help you move forward with confidence. Strengthening your base doesn't require perfection; it requires presence. It's the intentional work of reviewing your financial landscape, tightening up the loose ends, and preparing for what's ahead.

This principle reminds me of my son, who is an architect. I've watched him work through blueprints, soil tests, load calculations, and structural foundations long before the first wall is ever raised. He'll often say, "If the foundation isn't solid, nothing else matters." That stuck with me. In many ways, your financial life works the same way. You can dream of abundance and design a beautiful future, but if your financial footing is unstable, you'll always be one unexpected moment away from collapse.

Strengthening your base is about making sure your foundation can support what you're building. This focus includes creating habits that anchor you, such as checking your balances weekly, reviewing bills, organizing your accounts, and protecting your financial peace. It's not glamorous work, but it's grounding. When your foundation is strong, everything else begins to stabilize too: your emotions, your decisions, your ability to breathe. A strong base gives you the freedom to design a future that doesn't just look good, but one that lasts.

Stabilizing and strengthening your finances isn't

just about survival; it's about building a base strong enough to support your next level. When a house is built, the foundation determines how well it can weather storms. The same is true for your finances. Strengthening your financial base means creating consistency, building buffers, and developing systems that allow you to feel secure, not just today, but long-term. This begins with establishing a reliable rhythm: knowing what you earn, where it goes, and how much you keep. It may sound simple, but tracking your income and expenses consistently is a powerful act of ownership. It's in this phase that you put up guardrails by building an emergency fund, catching up on overdue bills, or finally putting your budget on paper. Every small step strengthens your sense of control and stability.

But strengthening also means preparing for what's ahead. Life is full of seasons-some bring growth, others bring disruption. A strong financial base allows you to handle both. That might mean saving for upcoming expenses, automating your financial system, or reducing your reliance on credit cards as a source of living. The stronger your base, the more confidently you can respond to unexpected events without derailing your progress.

In this phase, progress may not always feel exciting, but it's essential. The goal is stability. Strengthening your financial base is like fortifying your foundation with concrete. You're building strength, resilience, and readiness for everything that's to come. It's not flashy, but it's where true peace begins.

Reflection Questions:

1. In what ways is your current financial base strong, and where is it shaky?

2. What small action can you take this week to strengthen your financial foundation?

3. How would your life feel different if you felt fully stable and supported financially?

From Vision to Action: Setting Goals That Stick

Many women set goals out of fear, frustration, or urgency — not from a place of values, vision, and faith. When I finally put my financial structure in order, it required me to get clear on my vision, both personally and professionally. I had to shift from scattered effort to strategic, Spirit-led planning. That meant setting goals that were not only meaningful and purposeful but also practical and attainable in my current season.

I realized that big dreams aren't built only by big wins or large purchases. They can be achieved through small, consistent wins — the kind that seem simple but compound over time. The real key was consistency. Stabilizing your finances begins with short-term goals that are realistic, clear, and motivating. You may not be ready to save $10,000 or pay off your car this month, but you *can* save $250 in 30 days or reduce one bill.

Strategic goals are specific. Instead of saying, "I want to save," say, "I will save $25 from each paycheck for the next six weeks." Instead of "I want to get out of debt," say, "I will pay $50 extra toward my smallest card until it's gone." Specificity creates structure — and structure builds stability. When your goals are measurable, you can track your wins. Every finished savings challenge, every week you stick to your grocery budget, every time you log your expenses — it all counts. Those small victories build momentum and confidence.

Why Clarity is the First Breakthrough

"Write the vision and make it plain..." – Habakkuk 2:2

You cannot pursue what you haven't named, and you cannot reach what you haven't seen. This is why we begin with *vision casting*. Vision casting is the process of creating a clear mental picture of the future you desire — the kind of life you're working toward — and then setting meaningful goals to help you get there. Your vision should inspire and motivate you to take action, stay the course, and overcome obstacles along the way.

This vision becomes your *why*. It shapes your definition of success and keeps you focused on the steps needed to get there. For example, if your vision is to purchase a home, you may discover that you first need to raise your credit score to 650 or higher (700+ for better interest rates). That means your "buy a home" goal now contains a smaller goal: "Increase my credit score." Each major goal may have supporting goals and action steps within it.

The SMARTER P.A.T.H. Goal Framework

In ASCEND, we combine two powerful tools — the SMARTER method and the P.A.T.H. method — so your goals are not only clear and actionable, but also deeply aligned with your values and vision.

Step 1: Use SMARTER to Shape Your Goals *(the "how")*

SMARTER goals take your dreams from vague ideas to specific, measurable, and achievable steps:

- **S – Specific:** Clearly define what you want to achieve.
- **M – Measurable:** Determine how you will track progress.
- **A – Achievable:** Ensure the goal is realistic for your current resources and season.
- **R – Relevant/Related:** Align it with your values, vision, and faith.
- **T – Time-bound:** Give it a deadline to create urgency and focus.
- **E – Evaluate:** Regularly review your progress.
- **R – Readjust:** Make changes if your circumstances or priorities shift.

Setting SMARTER goals requires focus and reflection. This is not something to rush. Find a quiet, uplifting space — your "happy place" — and imagine yourself living the results you want to see in the timeframe you've set. From there, write goals that bridge where you are now to where you want to be.

Step 2: Follow the P.A.T.H. to Keep Them Aligned ***(the "why/what")***

While SMARTER tells you *how* to set your goals, P.A.T.H. ensures they reflect your deepest values and purpose, and not your fears. It is a deeper spiritual, strategic tool that allows you to:

- **P – Prioritize Your Values**

  Before we talk numbers, we talk about what matters. What do you value most? Freedom? Travel? Stability? Peace? Giving? Time with family? When you name what matters most, you make it easier to make decisions.

  Ask yourself: What do I truly want my money to do for me and for those I love?

- **A – Assess Your Reality**

  This is your financial check-in; no judgment, just honesty. How much do you actually bring in? Where is it going? Are your financial habits reflecting the life you want? Here is where you can also begin calculating your net worth, your honest financial snapshot. Don't be discouraged if you have not built a positive net worth at this point. Knowing your baseline is an act of power, not shame.

- **T – Target Aligned Goals**

  Now that your values and numbers are clear, it's time to aim intentionally. No more "I want to save more" or "I need to get out of debt someday." Let's make it plain: "I will save $1,000 for emergencies in 90 days; or I will pay off my credit card by December; or I will tithe consistently every month and track my giving." Your goals should match your purpose and not the pressure you are under.

- **H – Honor Your Next Step**

  This is the most overlooked part of goal setting — stewarding the next right move. You don't have to fix everything this month. You just need to honor your next assignment. That might be: creating your financial freedom spending plan, saying no to one unnecessary expense, or opening a money market savings account. Every step in alignment with your values counts. And obedience and consistency to the vision compound.

Aligning Your Spending with Your Values

Your money should reflect what matters most to you—not what the world says you should prioritize. Stabilization and strengthening invite you to take an honest look at where your money is going and ask: Is this aligned with the life I want to live?

Too often, we spend out of habit or pressure—buying things we think we need to feel accepted, important, or "caught up." But when you begin to align your spending with your values, your budget becomes a mirror of your priorities. That might mean spending less on the latest fashion and more on your health. Or skipping takeout so you can finally fund your daughter's dance class. This isn't about making you feel guilty; it's about choice. Every dollar has a destination. When you start directing it toward what fuels your joy, purpose, and peace, your entire financial journey becomes more sustainable. Your new money narrative is that you are no longer depriving yourself, you're designing your life. Stabilization doesn't mean you can't have what you love. It means you start being honest about what really matters, and you begin letting go of what doesn't.

When your values and your finances don't align, it creates more than frustration; it creates exhaustion. Many women are working, earning, and even succeeding outwardly, but inside, they feel drained and directionless. That's the cost of disconnection. Disconnected from their values and priorities of what is more important with the money you earn. They are moving in shame and guilt. How are you disconnected from your values?

Are you spending out of guilt? Hustling without a plan? Saying yes when your spirit says no? These are signs that something is off and that a shift is needed in your finances.

When you are disconnected from purpose, money becomes a stressor rather than a tool. And it's easy to get caught in cycles of busyness without progress (working extra hours but don't see the extra money in your bank account), taking home a biweekly check but a negative cash flow. That's why reconnecting your income to your purpose is not optional; it's essential.

Realigning begins with awareness. What matters most to you? Are your finances supporting or sabotaging that? As you go deeper, you'll discover that the cost of staying disconnected is too high; but the reward of realignment is peace, clarity, and sustainable prosperity.

Reflection Questions

1. What are three values that matter most to me—and does my current spending reflect them?

2. Where in my budget or habits am I spending out of pressure, guilt, or autopilot?

3. What is one change I can make this month to align my money with my priorities more deeply?

Dr. Juanita's Word of Truth

Stability is not a finish line-it's a foundation. With each step you take to build structure and order, you're declaring that chaos no longer has control over your finances. You're building peace that lasts.

As you stabilize and strengthen your finances, remember, you are laying bricks for the future you deserve. Stay committed to the basics, trust the process, and give yourself grace as you grow. Your roots are getting deeper and stronger.

Your Affirmation:

"I build my financial foundation with wisdom and strength. Every dollar I steward brings me closer to stability, peace, and freedom. My house is established on clarity, discipline, and God's wisdom, and it cannot be shaken."
(Anchored in Proverbs 24:3–4)

Transformation Spotlight

2. Danielle B. — Breaking Free from Debt & Shame

Starting Situation:

- Income: $10,000/month (Private Practice Physician)
- $120,000 in student loan debt + $18,000 in credit card debt
- Practice revenue was inconsistent, causing cash flow issues

- Embarrassed to ask for help—felt like a financial failure in private

Breakthrough Moment:
During "Eliminate What's Holding You Back," she acknowledged how shame had led to avoidance. She admitted that even with a high income, her finances were unstable because she hadn't built a financial system or reserve.

Transformation:

- Consolidated credit card debt with a low-interest loan
- Began weekly money check-ins and implemented a savings system for business and personal use.
- Created a faith-aligned giving plan and personal salary structure
- Reported feeling "liberated and honest" about her financial truth

Access Bonus Content from Dr. Juanita

Chapter 3

Control and Clarify Your Finances

"Wisdom is the principal thing; therefore get wisdom. And in all your getting, get understanding." — Proverbs 4:7

From Guessing to Knowing

"You don't have a money problem — you have a clarity problem." — Dr. Juanita Taylor

Have you ever found yourself working hard but still feeling stuck? Making money, but not making real progress? I did. And I found out that a lot of the women I coach are as well. They're reacting instead of leading. Spending instead of stewarding and surviving instead of building. Clarity changes that.

If you've ever felt like your paycheck vanishes before you even have time to enjoy it, you're not alone. I've coached women earning $40,000 a year and women earning six figures—and both have told me the same thing:

- "I make decent money, but I never know where it goes."

- "I'm tired of guessing if I have enough."
- "Every month feels like I'm just trying to stay afloat."

If that's you, you're not alone — and you're not bad with money. You're just missing what most of us were never taught: how to clearly manage cash flow.

The truth is, it's not always about how much you earn. It's about how much you keep, where it's going, and whether your spending aligns with your values and vision. That's the heart of *control*—not just knowing your numbers but directing them with purpose. This isn't about cutting back your lattes. This is about finally seeing your financial life with *honesty and authority.*

When I was silently struggling, I avoided truly looking at my finances because I feared what I'd see. But the moment I faced the truth, I felt lighter. Why? Because clarity removes fear. You stop feeling like money is in control of you, and you step into your rightful role as the one in charge.

Many women think they have a money problem, but what they really have is a visibility problem. If you don't know your numbers, you can't direct them. Knowing your cash flow is the rhythm of your financial life. It's the pattern of what's coming in versus what's going out.

Understanding your cash flow gives you power and control in your life. It reveals where you're overspending, where you can redirect funds, and where your money is serving (or sabotaging) your peace. Without this clarity, even high earners can feel broke, weighed down, and drowning.

This section isn't about judgment; it's about awareness. Whether your income is steady or unpredictable, seeing the full picture allows you to move with strategy instead of stress. Once you begin tracking and honoring your cash flow, you stop guessing and start leading. That's where financial freedom begins—not with more money, but with more clarity.

When it comes to financial freedom, clarity is power. Clarifying your cash flow means understanding exactly what's coming in, what's going out, and where your money is going. Many women feel financially overwhelmed, not because they don't earn enough, but because they don't have a clear picture of how their money is moving. Clarity takes the guesswork out of decision-making and replaces it with confidence. It shifts you from reactive to intentional, from scattered to structured.

Building a financial system takes clarity one step further. It's not just about knowing your numbers—it's about organizing them in a way that works for your life. This involves creating a system, something that I lacked previously. So, I put together a Financial Freedom Spending Plan (FFSP). This was my way of tracking my income, automating my savings, paying bills on time, and managing my spending without constantly stressing. Whether your income is steady or fluctuating, a system gives you a consistent rhythm. It helps you stay grounded, even when life gets hectic and unpredictable.

A Financial Freedom Spending Plan is designed based upon your life, your expenses, your income, your debts, and your savings. I call it a Financial Freedom Spending Plan because I wanted it to reflect what my goals were: spending in a way that moved me towards financial freedom. I chose not to say budget because that said to me that I could not spend my money, and it was restrictive to me. So, I wanted to tell my money how I wanted it to be spent. In essence, I gave my money roles and responsibilities that would lead me to freedom, abundance, and prosperity.

Your Financial Freedom Spending Plan will do the same for you. It doesn't have to be complicated. In fact, the simpler it is, the more likely you are to stick with it. What matters most is that it's clear, consistent, and customized to your lifestyle, your income and expenses, and your goals. It will give you visibility into your money, help you stay accountable, and support your financial goals—both short- and long-term.

Ultimately, having cash flow clarity and a strong FFSP free up more than just money; they free up mental space and time putting out fires in your life due to unplanned expenses. You don't have to live in anxiety, wondering if you missed a bill or spent too much. With your FFSP, you get clarity and structure, you make room for peace, purpose, and progress. You stop being managed by your money and start managing it with confidence.

This chapter is not about restriction; it's about freedom. We're going to:

- Track every dollar that flows in and out
- Build a spending plan that manages your financial life through a system that reflects your priorities
- Identify "sneaky leaks" and plug them

- Create financial spending categories and boundaries that protect your goals

By the time you finish, you'll have more than a budget, you'll have a Financial Freedom Spending Plan for your money, freedom, and prosperity.

I used to avoid looking at my numbers. Not because I didn't care, but because I didn't want to face the truth. I thought if I just worked harder, made more, and kept pushing forward, the stress would disappear. But the truth is, no amount of hustle can fix a lack of clarity. When I finally sat down and got honest with my cash

flow, I discovered it wasn't just about income-it was about intention.

You may be bringing in the income and making enough, but without clarity, it will never feel like enough. There will always be something that is taking your money. That is the devour that the Bible speaks of. (Malachi 3:11) It just goes, and many times you have no idea where it all went. You find yourself saying, "I thought I had more money than this; I thought I had a $20 bill somewhere in my purse". You might feel like you're spinning in circles, wondering where your money goes each month. The truth is, what we don't track, we can't transform.

What would it feel like to confidently know where every dollar is going? What if your money had a purpose-and a plan?

In this chapter, you'll learn how to get crystal clear on your cash flow so you can make intentional, informed financial decisions. We'll explore spending categories, create a flow plan that reflects your real life, and begin to shift from overwhelm to ownership, one number at a time.

Building Your Financial Freedom Spending Plan (FFSP) Zero-Based Method

A Financial Freedom Spending Plan (FFSP) is a form of a budget in simple terms. However, I do not call it a budget because a budget says to me restrictions on my spending. But the Financial Freedom Spending Plan tells me how to spend my money. I get to decide how much I want to spend and where I want to spend my dollars. It is not deprivation but rather spending with an intentional purpose.

An FFSP reflects your priorities and what's important to you. It includes grace for fun, a buffer for the unexpected, and structure that supports your values. This is where your financial decisions stop feeling restrictive and start feeling freeing.

You'll leave this section equipped to build your plan that aligns with both your finances and your dreams.

With a zero-based spending plan, your income minus your expenses should equal $0, not because you're broke, but because you're intentional and deliberate. This method eliminates the question, 'Where did my money go?' because every dollar is assigned a purpose: giving, saving, spending, debt repayment, vacation, etc. When you spend from a place of clarity, not chaos, you experience peace.

The goal of your FFSP isn't perfection, it's alignment. It ends every month with a positive balance, even if it's just one dollar. That single dollar means you earned more than you spent, and that's the beginning of building abundance.

Step One: Know Your True Income

The first courageous step to gaining clarity and control of your financial system is knowing your numbers. Knowing exactly how much money you bring in each month. You'd be surprised how many people don't actually know this number. Instead, we spend from a *blind place*—guessing, rounding, or assuming our income is one amount when it's actually another. The result? We often spend more than we're bringing in, either because:

- We think our income stretches further than it does, or
- We don't have a clear understanding of what our dollars can realistically cover.

This lack of clarity leads to negative balances, financial leaks, overdrafts, and financial stress.

Knowing your numbers means going beyond 'I think I make enough' or 'I don't know where it all goes' and looking directly at the facts. How much money is coming in—after taxes? What are your fixed bills? What do you actually spend on groceries, gas, subscriptions, childcare, or eating out? Until you lay it all out, you're operating from assumption—not clarity.

Start by listing every stream of income you receive in a month, including your job, side hustles, child support, and even irregular payments. Then list your expenses in categories: fixed (same each month), variable (changes monthly), and occasional (quarterly bills or annual fees). Include every dollar, even the little things like vending machines, late fees, or convenience charges. Every dollar has a story—and when you track it, that story becomes visible.

It might be uncomfortable at first, especially if you haven't done this in a while. But the discomfort is temporary. What comes next is power. Because once you know, you can adjust. You can stop leaking money, start creating breathing room, and shift your habits with intention.

Inflow: All Your Income Sources

- Primary job or salary
- Side hustle or freelance work
- Business income
- Child support or alimony
- Rental income
- Refunds, reimbursements, gifts

Understanding Fixed vs. Variable Expenses

When building your spending plan, it's essential to understand the difference between fixed and variable expenses—because how you treat them will impact how consistent and realistic your FFSP feels.

Fixed expenses are costs that typically stay the same from month to month, both in the amount and the due date. These are predictable, recurring payments that you can count on being part of your budget each cycle. Examples include:

- Rent or mortgage payments
- Car payments
- Insurance premiums
- Loan payments
- Certain subscriptions (such as streaming services or gym memberships)

Because they don't fluctuate much, fixed expenses are the easiest to plan for and usually form the backbone of your spending plan.

Variable expenses, on the other hand, change from month to month. The amount can vary based on usage, choices, or seasonal factors, and the timing of the expense may also shift. Examples include:

- Groceries

- Utilities*
- Dining out
- Medical costs
- Gas for your car
- Entertainment and discretionary spending

Variable expenses can be more challenging to allocate for because they're less predictable.

Outflow: All Your Expenses

- **Fixed Expenses** – predictable amount & due date every month (rent, insurance, savings/ Your Name, utilities).
- **Variable Expenses** – changes month to month (groceries, fuel, entertainment).
- **Irregular Expenses** – occasional but predictable (car repairs, holiday travel, annual memberships).

Why Utilities Are in My "Fixed" Category

While most people categorize utilities as variable, I recommend placing them in the fixed category. Here's why:

- Utility bills can swing dramatically depending on the season.
- In summer, high electricity usage from running the air conditioner can spike your bill to $300–$600 or more.

- In winter, heating costs can cause your gas bill to climb sharply.

If you don't plan ahead for these seasonal changes, you may find yourself short on funds, reaching for a credit card, or skipping other bills to cover the difference—disrupting your entire spending plan.

Instead, take your total annual cost for electricity and gas and divide each by 12 to find your "average" monthly amount. Plan for that amount year-round. When your bill is lower, the extra you've paid creates a credit on your account. When the bill is higher, that credit helps cover the difference without derailing your plan.

This method smooths out seasonal spikes, keeps your FFSP steady, and removes the stress of surprise utility bills.

Fixed vs. Variable Expenses Table

Category	Description	Examples
Fixed Expenses	Costs that stay the same each month in both amount and due date.	Rent/Mortgage, Car Payment, Insurance Premiums, Loan Payments, Memberships
Variable Expenses	Costs that change monthly based on usage, season, or choice.	Groceries, Utilities*, Dining Out, Medical Costs, Fuel, Entertainment

Utility Averaging Formula Worksheet

Annual Electric Bill Total: $________ ÷ 12 = $________ monthly
Annual Gas Bill Total: $________ ÷ 12 = $________ monthly

Step 2: Track Every Dollar

Tracking your income and expenses is like taking inventory of your life. It may feel tedious at first, but it's one of the most empowering financial actions you can take. Think of it another way, it's like turning on the lights in a dark room—you can't fix what you can't see.

Before you can take control, you need the full picture. You deserve to know where your money is going. We address our finances and make decisions based on a lack of knowledge. Many don't know how much they have coming in and, more importantly, how much is going out.

Start by reviewing the past 30-60 days of credit card and bank statements. Write down every dollar that came in and every dollar that went out—fixed bills, variable costs, random purchases, and yes, those sneaky financial leaks as well. This data is your truth, no judgment, just honesty.

Most women are shocked by what they discover: the number of Starbucks runs, the amount spent at the gas station for snacks or restaurants, along with the high grocery bill. It's not about guilt—it's about revelation. When you see where your money goes, you can begin to redirect it toward what matters most or make adjustments in needed areas/categories.

This habit, repeated monthly, becomes a financial mirror. And when you look clearly in that mirror, you can stop avoiding, start adjusting, and step into ownership with confidence. You begin to see your spending for what it is and stop hiding and release the shame.

Create a Flow Plan

Once you know your numbers, the next step is to direct them with intention. A flow plan is a strategic method for deciding how your income will move, when it will move, and where it will move to so that it makes the most impact.

This includes setting clear spending categories and summarizing your expenses to stay balanced, consistent, and timely with your expenses and goals.

Start with your income schedule—map out when your paychecks arrive, then align those dates with the bills and obligations due throughout the month. This helps you distribute your income across the month wisely, avoiding overwhelm in high-expense weeks. Your flow plan should include due dates, payment amounts, and designated income sources to cover each item.

Then, track your spending for 1–3 months to capture your complete financial picture. Use your **Fixed & Variable Expense Tracker** to organize your spending into Spending Categories and assign each category a monthly spending amount.

You can visit the toolbox for this tracker and a detailed list of additional resources at the end of this book.

Create your Spending Categories so that they reflect your lifestyle. Common categories include: Essentials,

Financial Goals, Flexible Spending, Giving + Tithing, and Saving Buckets.

Once you've built your categories, it's time to create your Expense Summary and Calendar. This is a snapshot of your expenses and their due dates over a 30-day period, organized by category to reveal patterns and guide your flow plan decisions.

This process transforms budgeting into purpose-driven spending planning.

Your spending categories become boundaries that protect your goals, and your expense summary becomes a mirror that reflects your habits.

From Deficit to Abundance

One of the most effective ways to shift from a deficit to abundance is by creating **spending categories**. These categories group your purchases into specific areas and assign a monthly dollar limit to each.

Example Spending Categories:

- **Housing:** Rent/Mortgage, Home Insurance, HOA dues, Maintenance
- **Automobile:** Car Payment, Gas, Maintenance, Insurance
- **Utilities:** Electric, Gas, Water, Trash, Internet, Phone
- **Education:** Tuition, Books, Fees, School Lunches

- **Food:** Groceries, Dining Out, Coffee/Lunch Purchases
- **Entertainment:** Movies, Events, Subscriptions
- **Saving Buckets / Goals**

By setting a specific dollar amount for each category, you gain control over your spending instead of letting it control you. You should assign every dollar of your income a role and responsibility.

Step 3: Complete Your Expense Summary Snapshot

Know the Details of Your Expenses

When tracking your expenses, go beyond just listing the name and amount. For each item, record:

- **Account Number**
- **Monthly Amount Due**
- **Due Date**
- **Interest Rate** (if applicable)

This information gives you a full picture of your obligations and helps you spot opportunities to save or negotiate.

◊ For your **Expense Summary and Calendar**, visit the **Quick Reference Toolbox at the End of the book.**

Complete your Expenses Summary and Expense Calendar that includes:

- **Category** (Housing, Transportation, Food, Debt, Savings, Giving, Personal, Seasonal)
- **Monthly Amount**
- **Due Date**
- **Payment Method** (auto-pay, manual)

This becomes your quick-reference money map.

Step 4: Build Your Cash Flow Calendar

Many money problems aren't about *amounts*—they're about *timing*. If most of your bills are due before your second paycheck, you'll always feel like you're behind.

- List your pay dates for the month.
- Add each bill with its due date and amount.
- See where you need to shift payment dates or set aside money from the first check to cover the second-half bills.

It is also helpful to divide your bills up based on the number of pay periods you have each month. For example, if you are paid biweekly, then divide your bills by 2. That way, you are paying half of each bill from each check. This allows for your payroll deposit to stretch further. Your housing expenses and automobile expenses usually are the largest expenses for the month. This way if your mortgage/ rent is $1200, you only pay $600 per pay period instead of the whole $1200 at the beginning of the month. I remember when I first got out of college, I would pay my rent from my first check of the month and would be basically broke until the next check came. If I had followed this system back then, I probably would not have felt as stressed each month until my second check came in.

Now, this system is best when you are a month ahead of your bills. This way, for instance, your January payroll deposits cover February's expenses, and February payroll deposits cover March's expenses, and so on and so forth. Having a system such as this allows you to make adjustments easier to your Financial Freedom Spending Plan. And, you will also have the dollar amount needed for next month's expenses ahead of time. This way, you will be able to see if you need to cut out some of your extracurricular activities or entertainment ahead of time, or even work extra hours if that is an option.

Step 5: Complete Your Financial Freedom Spending Plan Form

Complete your FFSP form (Visit for your copy of your FFSP form.)

Steps to Create your FFSP

1. Determine your total monthly income. Include all sources of income (alimony, side hustles, child support, etc.)

2. Total your fixed expenses for the month. Please include your utilities as a fixed expense and pay a set amount each month to prevent going over your allotted amount for each spending category. Subtract the total amount of fixed expenses from your total income for the month.

3. Determine and total all periodic expenses for the year, and average the amount by dividing by twelve to get a set monthly amount that you will put into your fixed expense spending amount. Subtract from the balance of income remaining.

4. Determine and total your variable expenses for the month. In this category, you may introduce the Envelope System or a designated bank account for certain spending categories such as groceries, car gas, entertainment, or weekly lunches. Subtract from the remaining balance. At this point in your plan, you should determine if you have a positive (+) or negative (-) balance of income remaining. If you have a (+) balance, you will have income to be used in the next section of the FFSP for debt reduction and/ or your savings buckets (dreams and

goals).

5. If you have debt, you will determine a "debt reduction dollar amount" that you will pay on your debt to speed the process of paying your debt off. You may use the entire (+) balance, or you may use a percentage of it for your debt reduction and a percentage towards your dreams and goals. If you have a (-) balance, you will have to eliminate some items in your spending plan or decrease the dollar amount that you have allotted for each variable expense spending category until you get to a (+) balance. It may take you a few attempts to get this part figured out. But you should continue to look at different scenarios until you can get to a (+) balance. Sometimes you may have to decrease some items, and sometimes you may have to get additional income into the equation.

6. For decreasing your debts, you will decide whether to use the debt snowball method or the debt avalanche method as part of your Debt Reduction Plan. You will include all expenses that will eventually have a zero balance.

7. The Dreams, Goals, and Saving Bucket part of the FFSP is the fun zone. Here, you get to decide on dollar amounts to place into your dreams, goals, and savings. If you do not have a Life Happens Emergency Savings Plan, it is recommended that you fund this savings bucket first. This will allow you to have some sort of contingency plan when life happens. It is also not recommended to do elaborate vacations until you have gotten your debt structure into a manageable and healthy state.

Your FFSP is unique to you and your finances and goals. Remember to draw from your "Why" as it will help to keep you committed to the process. This is not an easy journey, but it is DEFINITELY worth taking!

Positive vs. Negative Balances

Here's the simplest way to see it:

- **Positive Balance (Surplus/Abundance):** Your income is greater than your expenses. *(Income – Expenses = Positive Number)*
- **Negative Balance (Deficit):** Your expenses are greater than your income. *(Income – Expenses = Negative Number)*

Positive Balance: This is where you have options for your money. Your previously set goals and dreams can now be aligned with your finances when you have money left over at the end of the month. Having a positive balance allows you an opportunity to be in control of your destiny and finances. The positive balance will be used to fund your Savings Buckets: goals, dreams, debt reduction, and/ or establishing emergency funds.

When there is a positive balance, those dollars are not just extra dollars left over, but see them as the keys to your financial freedom, your prosperity, and your abundance. The positive balance will be used to fund one of your spending categories or your Savings Buckets: goals, dreams, debt reduction, and/ or establishing emergency funds.

Negative Balance: Having a negative balance isn't

the end of the world. It does, however, mean that you have some more work to do to dig your way out of the negative to the positive. If you currently have a negative balance, don't be discouraged. Creating your Financial Freedom Spending Plan allows you to adjust and modify your expenses to move toward a surplus. This is also a great motivation to stay focused and targeted with your FFSP to reduce the chances of you landing back into the negative balance.

Strategies to Decrease Your Negative Balance

Increase your income: Maybe you work four days a week and you are able to increase to five days a week, or weekends, or evenings. Maybe you do some services for family members that you may be paid for through family members or outside of the family, such as cleaning or decluttering services. Maybe you enjoy cooking and can prepare meals for families or individuals.

Decrease your spending: This is usually the step that makes the biggest difference in your Financial Freedom Spending Plan. Setting an amount for the items you want to purchase and staying within the boundaries of that category for a few months. You may also be able to cut down on the number of times you eat out and set a timer for your furnace or air conditioner to be on at the times that you are at home.

Eliminate late fees and overdraft fees: Creating a Financial Freedom Spending Plan allows you to decrease and eliminate late fees and delinquent or overdraft fees that you are paying because you will be on a schedule for when your payments are to be made. And because you use the deposits from the prior month as the funds to be used for the current month's expenses, you are able to know what dollar amounts need to be in your account, so there is less chance for late fees or overdraft fees.

Use of the Envelop System or Bank account designated for miscellaneous spending: Placing cash or a debit card for dedicated miscellaneous spending, such as car gas, eat-out food, hair products, spontaneous entertainment, or unplanned purchases, allows for fewer chances of spending your monthly expenses. You are more in control of your spending this way because you can see how much money you have available for this type of spending. Recognizing that you only have, for example $50 left over for the remaining two weeks of the month for entertainment, helps you to be more selective about the types of entertainment you are able to do and how often you can do that sort of entertainment.

For example, if you want to go out to eat with your girls and they suggest Cheesecake Factory, but you only have Wendy's money, you may not be able to accompany them on that evening out. This prevents using your monthly expense money for unplanned spending or outings. And this does not mean that this will always be your scenario. But after you have been able to get your balance to a positive one, you are then better prepared to make decisions and choices on these types of spending or outings.

Decrease Amounts Designated for your Variable Expenses: The Financial Freedom Spending Plan is designed so that you set amounts available for each spending category. You have the autonomy to change and adjust amounts to make them work for your spending needs on the variable expense spending accounts. For some of the fixed expenses, you may be able to decrease the amounts, such as credit cards, for which you will be paying the minimal amounts due for those accounts that you are not paying off at that time. You may also decrease your utility bills by setting them up as a fixed expense that will allow you to build credit on the account, or even by having the utility company place you in a budget-pay option.

Sometimes, there just isn't enough money, and if this is you, then you will need to focus on keeping the situation from getting bigger. Sometimes your scenario may require bigger and more drastic lifestyle adjustments, such as moving to a smaller home or apartment, selling a car, getting a roommate, or a second job. Bigger lifestyle adjustments will require more planning and more time, of course. A less drastic adjustment is to continue to work through your Financial Freedom Spending Plan and debt reduction to find boundaries that will put money back into your bank accounts.

Certain expenses should be a top priority. Ask yourself what will happen if you don't pay an expense such as your rent or mortgage? Could you be evicted or foreclosed? Will utilities be shut off? Will your wages be garnished? Always pay expenses for housing, and those who will bring legal action against you if they are not paid. Then focus on expenses that will result in fines and late fees if they are not paid on time. Avoid using loans, if at all possible. To pay monthly expenses, especially those with high interest rates. This can make your scenario worse and make it more difficult to pay future expenses.

Be patient with yourself through this process and keep making adjustments and trying! Building a Financial Freedom Spending Plan is a process, not a one-time event. Check your plan often and make necessary changes to help it fit your scenario. The more you work on it, the better it will work for you!

Sample Financial Freedom Spending Plan:

Categories	**Budget**	**Actual**
Income Sources		
__________	__________	__________
__________	__________	__________
__________	__________	__________
Total Income		
Fixed Expenses	Budget	Actual
Categories		
__________	__________	__________
__________	__________	__________
__________	__________	__________
__________	__________	__________
__________	__________	__________

Subtotal	______	______
Balance Remaining	______	______
Periodic Expenses	Budget	Actual
Categories		
______	______	______
______	______	______
______	______	______
______	______	______
______	______	______
Subtotal	______	______
Balance Remaining	______	______
Variable Expenses	Budget	Actual
Categories		
______	______	______
______	______	______
______	______	______
______	______	______
______	______	______
Subtotal	______	______

+ / - Balance Remaining __________ __________

Debt Reduction Plan	Budget	Actual
Debt Reduction $ Amt.	__________	__________
__________	__________	__________
__________	__________	__________
__________	__________	__________
__________	__________	__________
__________	__________	__________
Subtotal	__________	__________
Balance Remaining	__________	__________

Dreams/Goals/Savings Buckets	Budget	Actual
Categories		
__________	__________	__________
__________	__________	__________
__________	__________	__________
__________	__________	__________
__________	__________	__________

Subtotal	____________	____________
Final Amount	____________	____________
Total Income	____________	
Minus		
Total Expenses	____________	
Equals (+)	____________	or (-) ____________

Step 6: Create your Debt Reduction Plan (DRP)

Before you can create your Debt Reduction Plan, you should take some time to write your unique debt story. Your debt tells a story about you and your spending habits. If you are completely honest with yourself, you will see that a lot of your debt accumulation may have been from emotional spending, or keeping up with social media, or poor money management, or excessive overspending. Either way, your debt should paint a picture of your "debt story". It's important to understand the decisions that were made surrounding your debt to help you not make the same decisions again that could lead you back into a "debt-driven journey".

How does your debt make you feel? Anger, sadness, frustration, shame, and/or guilt. Capturing your emotions surrounding your debt is huge to help you stay the course for debt elimination. Debt elimination is a journey, just as seeking financial freedom and prosperity is a journey.

Creating your unique debt story is more than listing

numbers on a page—it's about uncovering the emotions and patterns that shaped your financial journey. When you understand why you spend the way you do, you begin to see the connections between your habits, your mindset, and your money choices. Embracing your story with honesty allows you to release shame, take ownership, and create a plan that feels personal and empowering. This deeper awareness becomes the anchor that helps you stay focused and resilient throughout your debt elimination journey.

After you have your income and expenses for your FFSP, it is time to decide how to eliminate your debt from your life. Just because you can afford something doesn't mean you have to buy it. To keep debt from accumulating unnecessarily, consider if something is a need or a want before you buy it, or give yourself a 24-hour waiting period before making debt purchases.

You will need to decide on an amount that you can commit to monthly as a debt reduction amount. This dollar amount ideally comes from the (+) balance or surplus that you have left over when you built your FFSP. You can be as aggressive as you like with this amount. It is set as a fixed expense in your FFSP. Contribute the budgeted amount towards your DRP every month and then track your debt balances to make sure that you pay down as much debt as you have planned. Once you pay it off your debt, it frees up your emotions and your finances to be able to fund your savings buckets with less restriction and stress.

You can visit the toolbox for a detailed list of additional resources at the end of this book.

Step 7: Make Routine Financial Check-Ins a Habit

Money management isn't a once-a-month activity; it's a rhythm of intentional and deliberate decisions regarding how your money should flow. Such as:

- Set a 15-minute "Money Date" each week or month.
- Review your transactions.
- Adjust for upcoming expenses.
- Celebrate small wins.

Routine check-ins also allow you to spot the "sneaky leaks" from your account. These are small expenses that silently drain your finances, such as subscriptions you forgot about or frequent drive-through stops; "it was on sale purchases", auto-renewals for unused services that you forgot about, banking fees, and direct deposit early withdrawals. You should do a subscription audit every 6 months and cancel or pause what you are not using or need. You would be surprised by the amount of money you may save.

When I first did this exercise, I was enlightened to the fact that I was still paying for cable boxes even though my children are grown, finished college, and no longer living at my home. With the SMART TVs, there was no need to continue to pay that fee for the times that my children would be staying over. It was much cheaper and more cost-effective to upgrade my TVs to all SMART TVs and use subscriptions that I already had when they visited, or allow them to use the subscriptions they had to log into the TV.

Step 8: Set and Honor Financial Boundaries

Boundaries are bridges to peace. Without them, your finances are vulnerable to impulse, pressure, and emotional spending. And your FFSP without boundaries is like a fence with a broken gate. I believe it's a tragedy to get out of your bed and hustle into work every day and make money and not take into consideration you, the future you, and your dreams and goals, and spend your money without factoring you into the equation. Ask yourself:

- Where do I overspend?
- Who or what tempts me to spend outside my plan?
- What purchase patterns feel emotional or impulsive?

Your FFSP means nothing if you don't respect your boundaries. This is where your values meet your wallet. This is where you reclaim the right to say 'no' where it matters. Maybe it's saying no to overspending on gifts, dining out, or bailing others out at your own expense. Maybe it's creating a spending limit that protects your savings goal. Boundaries aren't about restriction, they're about respect for you, your finances, and the future "you".

Honor starts with clarity. Identify where you tend to leak peace in your finances. Then draw a boundary—

not just on paper, but in practice. Commit to boundaries that align with your goals. For example, "I won't spend over $50 on dining out each week" or "I won't make any purchases over $100 without a 24-hour pause". When you honor your boundaries, you build trust in yourself. That self-trust becomes the foundation for bigger financial decisions in the future.

Step 9: Automate and Organize

Consistency creates stability—and automation supports consistency. Once your plan is in place, take the extra step to automate as much of it as possible. That means scheduling automatic bill pay, setting up recurring transfers to savings, and using calendar reminders for due dates. Automation protects your peace of mind and reduces the risk of missed payments or emotional overspending.

Next, organize the tools that support your plan. Create labeled folders—digital or physical—for receipts, financial documents, and account logins. Set a specific day each week (e.g., 'Money Monday') to check in on your progress. The more consistent your system, the less mental energy it will require to manage your money.

This is also where financial routines are born. Your system might include reviewing your accounts every Friday morning, updating your budget on Sundays, or checking your financial focus plan twice a month. When your system fits your rhythm, it becomes sustainable.

Most importantly, remember that your system is meant to serve you—not the other way around. You can always simplify, refine, or adjust. The goal isn't perfection. It's peace and freedom.

Step 10: Track your Progress and Celebrate

Keep motivation visible. Color in a chart each week you stay within your budget. Small visual wins keep you engaged for the long haul. Celebrate wins, but be sure not to get into more financial strains with your celebrations. Celebration is not just spending money, but it can be as simple as a Facebook post in the community, congratulating yourself on staying the course, or making adjustments to your FFSP that keep you on track with achieving a goal.

Align Spending With Values

Money is a mirror—and how you spend it reveals what you value. But here's the hard truth: many of us spend money in ways that don't reflect who we truly are or what we truly want.

Maybe you value peace, but overspend on things that create pressure. Maybe you value freedom, but are locked in impulsive purchases. This section helps you examine the disconnect.

When you realign your spending with your values, everything changes. Your money becomes a tool, not a trigger. Your purchases become intentional, not emotional.

This is about conscious stewardship. It's about using your dollars to build the life, legacy, and impact that matter most to you. That's clarity and controlled finances, and it's powerful.

Cash Flow Clarity Exercise

1. What is your total income this month?
2. What are your fixed and variable expenses?
3. Are your money habits aligned with your values?
4. What boundary do you need to protect this month?
5. How will you check in with your FFSP regularly?

Connect with Dr. Juanita on social pages by visiting her website AskDrJuanita.com

Dr. Juanita's Word of Truth

Clarity is power. This chapter is not about cutting out joy in your life; it's about directing your dollars so they serve you, the future you, and your dreams and goals. When you take charge of your cash flow, you're no longer guessing; you're leading. Every dollar you track, every plan you make, moves you closer to financial freedom, abundance, and prosperity.

You are not afraid of the numbers; you are mastering them. Keep clarifying, keep planning, and keep choosing to be intentional. Your money is no longer leading you. You are in control now.

Let's keep ASCENDING.

Your Affirmation

"I am no longer in the dark about my money. My expenses have been identified, my income verified, and I walk in clarity, truth, and discipline. I control my cash flow with peace and purpose, and every choice I make reflects alignment with my values and vision. My finances no longer direct me, I am in control of my finances."
(Anchored in Luke 14:28)

Transformational Spotlight

Renee L. — From Confused to Confident

Starting Situation:

- Income: $4,600/month (HR Manager, single mom of two)

- Had no budget system, only tracked income and bills mentally
- Frequently said "I don't know where my money goes"
- Felt stuck in survival mode and afraid of dreaming big

Breakthrough Moment:
Upon clarifying her cash flow, Renee completed her Net Worth and Expenses Summary. Seeing the actual numbers opened her eyes. She wasn't irresponsible; she was unstructured. That realization changed everything.

Transformation:

- Started budgeting using the ASCEND cash flow worksheet
- Paid off two credit cards totaling $1,400
- Opened a savings account for her kids and began saving $100/month
- Dream goal: purchase a home within 2 years—now feels it's possible

Chapter 4

Eliminate Debt Strategically

"The rich rule over the poor, and the borrower is slave to the lender." Proverbs 22:7 NIV

There's a heaviness that comes with financial pressure, not just in the bills or the balances, but in the weight of shame, regret, and the silence we often carry. I didn't realize how much I was dragging behind me until I tried to move forward. From debt to guilt to decisions I wish I could do over, I had to learn that you cannot rise while holding on to what's been weighing you down.

Maybe you've been there too, making strides, but feeling stuck. You've tried to move forward, but something keeps pulling you back. Often, it's not just the debt, it's the mindset surrounding your debt. The emotional and spiritual clutter around money must be cleared before you can elevate into peace, purpose, and prosperity.

What are you still carrying that's keeping you from rising? What would freedom look like if you finally let go?

I encourage you to take a powerful look at what needs to be released in your life, financially, emotionally, and spiritually. You'll discover how to eliminate draining habits, reduce debt, and break free from toxic cycles that keep you small and have a negative banking balance and little cash flow. It's time to clear the clutter, release the debt, and claim the space you were meant to rise into. It's time to move to abundance and peace.

Shame, Silence, and the Debt Burden

Debt is not just financial—it's emotional. It carries guilt, shame, secrecy, and even identity. So many women, even successful ones, are secretly drowning in credit card bills, student loans, business debt, and emotional spending… all while smiling on the outside and leading in their workplace or community. Many of them feel like failures because of their debt, even though the circumstances that led to it were often complex and reasonable.

I've been there. I know what it's like to juggle payments and pray for miracles.
To feel embarrassed about what I owed, even though I had every reason for why it happened. I've walked this road myself. As I shared earlier, there was a season when debt felt like a shadow I couldn't outrun. After closing my third dental practice, the financial strain was real, and the pressure was relentless. The weight of debt pressed in from every side. My mornings would often begin before sunrise, and my mind would race over how I would show up for the day and move through it as if I had no worries. The shame of not being "further along" and the quiet guilt of knowing something in my system wasn't working became constant companions.

I knew I couldn't continue on like this. It became very important to eliminate my debt burden. I told myself, this is not where my story ends. That whisper became my lifeline. And because I didn't want to revisit this space again and feel what I was feeling, I vowed to myself to get my strategy lined up and my systems in place. I decided instead of running and ignoring my debt story to face my reality, change my patterns, heal my financial chaos, and rebuild in a way that aligned my income with my purpose and direction of financial freedom and abundance. That decision didn't erase my debt overnight, but it gave me back my power. And out of that turning point, the ASCEND journey and framework were born.

This section is where we name your emotional weight; where you define your "debt story" and begin to release it. You are not your debt. You are not irresponsible or broken. You are a woman who deserves a plan, peace, and prosperity.

We break the silence by bringing debt into the light with compassion. Whether it's credit cards, student loans, or back taxes, this chapter begins with grace.

Because freedom doesn't begin with payoff—it begins with a decision to face the truth without shame and move forward with wisdom.

But let me say this clearly: debt carries more than just a balance; it carries **baggage, heavy, shameful baggage**. If left unaddressed, it becomes a cycle of repeating the same mistakes and making the same spending decisions that lead you to this place in the first place. And cycles don't break with shame; they break with strategy. You don't conquer debt by ignoring it. As long as I was hiding in my room in the evenings, I still had the mountain of debt I was trying to climb. You conquer it by naming it, facing it, and planning your exit. As long as I was hiding in my room in the evenings, I still had the mountain of debt I was trying to climb. It wasn't until I came up with a strategy of how to navigate the climb that I found and felt relief. Debt is not a moral failure. It is a financial circumstance, and you are not stuck there. This chapter is about getting clear, getting organized, and getting free.

Know Your Numbers

Clarity is the first step to freedom. Knowing your debt numbers—every balance, interest rate, and minimum payment—gives you the full picture you need to create a plan. It gives you your "Debt Story". It is important to walk through a simple yet powerful process: writing it all down and getting it out in the open. Not to panic, but to plan. When you avoid your debt, it grows in the dark. But when you face it with honesty, you take the first step toward conquering it. Information is not your enemy, it's your starting line. Every ending has to have a beginning, and this is your beginning. Once you do this, you will be equipped with a full debt snapshot and empowered to take your next step—one that feels clear and doable.

Choose Your Strategy: Snowball vs. Avalanche

There's no one 'right' way to pay off debt—but there is a best way for you. There are two effective methods of eliminating debt very strategically. They are The Debt Snowball Method and The Debt Avalanche

Method. The process for each is the same: you just decide your starting point, either by the lowest balance or the highest interest rate.

The Snowball Method helps you build momentum by paying off your smallest balances first. Each win boosts your confidence and motivation. I used the Snowball Method. I needed to know that something was happening fast in my debt journey. Once I put my numbers on paper and looked at them, I actually could afford to pay off several small debts right away. Through my coaching program, I have noticed this to be true for many of the women I have worked with. Many of them had debts of less than $1000 and could afford to pay them off right away as well. This gives the momentum that you need to get started and solidifies that it is possible to pay off your debt.

The Avalanche Method tackles your highest-interest debt first, saving you money in the long run. But putting both methods on paper and seeing which one is most effective for your situation. You'll explore both approaches and determine which one aligns with your personality and season in your journey. It's not about impressing anyone, it's about finding a path that keeps you moving. Once you choose your method, you'll learn how to build a simple but strategic plan to start eliminating debt, one payment at a time. I can say that for my business debt, I chose to use the Avalanche Method for some of the debts because of the amount of money it allowed me to save. You may choose to use a combination of the two methods, and that is perfectly fine. What matters most is that you choose a plan to get started with and stick to it.

Build a Roll-Down Plan

Speaking from my journey, the Snowball Method allowed me to create a roll-down plan, as I like to reference it. Debt freedom is a journey, and the roll-down plan is your vehicle. Each time you pay off a debt, you roll that payment into the next one. This creates a snowball effect that accelerates your progress and rolls down the debt mountain that you have.

In creating your personal roll-down plan, you'll list your debts in order, track your monthly progress, and watch momentum build with each win. There's power in progress, no matter how small. And when you consistently roll payments forward, what once felt like an impossible mountain to climb begins to feel like just a bump in the road because you get to see the height of your debt story mountain start to lower itself one payment at a time.

This is how you build financial confidence—not just through big steps, but through consistent movement uphill.

Plan for Progress, Not Perfection

You don't need a perfect income or perfect plan to eliminate debt. You just need consistency. Maybe you can't put $500 toward debt this month—but what about $25? That small step is still movement. And movement builds momentum. Now, as you know, life is life, and even though you designed your perfect plan, things happen that derail your plan. That is when you have to adjust your strategy as life gets hard, and learn how to celebrate the steps that count even when they feel small.

This is a good example of when you may need to use a combination of the two methods to accomplish your goal. Freedom is not about arriving all at once; it's about refusing to quit. This is your reminder that every step toward debt freedom is a victory.

Eliminate Debt Strategically

The Two Repayment Methods

The Debt Snowball Method

- Pay off your debts from **smallest to largest balance**.
- Focus on building **momentum and motivation**.
- Each win gives you a confidence boost.

Best for: Emotional progress, people who need to feel wins early.

The Debt Avalanche Method

- Pay off debts starting with the **highest interest rate**.
- Focuses on **mathematical efficiency** and long-term savings.
- You pay less interest over time.

Best for: Logical thinkers, long-term planners, and those with high-interest debt.

Which is better? Whichever one you will stay consistent with. Both work. Choose the one that works for your spirit and season.

1. **Your "Debt Reality Check"**

Take a deep breath, open your heart — and write it down:

- List every debt you have
- Include: balance, interest rate, minimum payment
- Choose your repayment strategy (Snowball or Avalanche)

Example:

Creditor	Interest Rate	Min. Payment
Credit Card A	24%	$45
Student Loan	6%	$120
Credit Card B	17%	$30
Car Loan	5%	$250

2. **Build Your Strategic Repayment Plan**

- Which debt will you attack first?
- What extra amount can you add monthly to your top-priority debt? This amount will come from

your (+) balance of your FFSP.

- What will you do with that freed-up money once it's paid off?

Let me introduce you to one of my clients. This is Nechelle telling her own Debt Story.

Nechelle's Debt Story: From Overwhelmed to Focused with the FFSP

Nechelle, a 38-year-old single mother of two, works full-time as a medical office administrator. After a difficult divorce and a short period of unemployment, she found herself buried in debt, juggling multiple credit cards, a car loan, a student loan, and her mortgage. When I met with Nechelle, this is what she shared with me:

"When I first sat down to face my finances, I was overwhelmed. My paycheck always seemed to disappear, and I was carrying balances across multiple credit cards, loans, and a mortgage. I had no system for where my money was going; I just knew I was tired of the stress."

I began working with Nechelle on creating her Financial Freedom Spending Plan and Debt Reduction Plan. Within two months, Nechelle had a completed FFSP to begin her journey. Here's her debt Story:

1. Credit Card A – $1,200 @ 24% (min. $45)
2. Credit Card C – $2,500 @ 19% (min. $75)
3. Credit Card B – $3,000 @ 21% (min. $90)

4. Credit Card D – $4,200 @ 17% (min. $125)

5. Car Loan – $9,500 @ 6% (min. $300)

6. Student Loans – $18,000 @ 5% (min. $200)

7. Mortgage – $140,000 @ 4% (min. $1,050)

Nechelle chose the Snowball method to pay off her debts because she needed emotional wins to stay motivated in the process, especially in the first year. Seeing her first debts disappear in just a few months kept her committed to the process.

Nechelle would pay all minimum payments on all cards and direct her debt reduction amount of $379 toward Credit Card A first because it had the lowest card balance of the four cards.
Once it was paid off, she rolled that $45 minimal payment plus $379 debt reduction amount into the payment for Credit Card C, which was the second lowest balance of the four cards, creating a bigger payment and faster payoff.

Nechelle's Results at the time of writing this book:

- First win in 3 months established her Life Happens Emergency Fund of $1137

- Paid off Credit Card A in three months following establishing her Life Happens Fund.

- Payoff of Credit Card C in 8 months

- Credit Card B was paid off in 14 months

- Every payoff built her confidence and freed more cash flow to allow her to move to Credit Card D and then her other debts.

Let's walk through Nechelle's numbers step-by-step so you can see exactly what her debt reduction amount allowed her to do and how it snowballed forward faster.

Establishing Life Happens Emergency Fund & Paying Off Credit Card A in 3 Months

- $379 times 3 months = $1137 (it is recommended to have between $1000 -$2000)
- Credit Card A Balance: $1,200
- Interest Rate: 24%
- Minimum Payment: $45/month

To pay it off in **3 months**, Nechelle needed to cover:

1. The **principal** ($1,200)
2. The **interest** over those 3 months (about $24/ month, ~$72 total)

Total to pay off in 3 months ≈ **$1,272.**
Dividing over 3 months: **$424/month.**

Since the minimum payment was $45, Nechelle put an extra $379/month toward Credit Card A. The $379 was the (+) balance that she discovered after completing her FFSP. She decided to use the whole amount towards debt reduction and establishing her emergency funds. She initially put the whole amount in her Life Happens Fund for the first three months for a total of $1137 and then shifted it to her Debt Reduction Plan in month four. This way, she had a little cushion to fall back on in case something happened and she didn't want to not have any money saved up.

Snowballing to Credit Card C

Once Credit Card A was gone, Nechelle freed up the $424/month she was paying ($45 minimum + $379 debt reduction amount = $424 total payment amount). She then took the $424 and added it to Credit Card C's $75 minimum payment.

- **Credit Card C Balance:** $2,500
- **Interest Rate:** 19%
- **Minimum Payment:** $75/month
- **New Payment with Snowball:** $424 + $75 = **$499/month**

At $499/month, she paid off $2,500 in 8 months.

Nechelle's Reflection

"The turning point came when I created my Financial Freedom Spending Plan (FFSP). For the first time, I listed all of my income, every expense, and gave every dollar a job. I finally had a clear picture of what I was working with. Seeing my expenses written

out for the first time like that showed me where my money was going and where I could use my (+) balance to make a difference in my finances. I created my very first emergency fund ever, the Life Happens Fund, and began to work on the 3-6 month Emergency Fund.

At first, these buckets only had a few dollars in them, but knowing they were there made me feel like I was finally planning for the future and getting my life on track. I felt like I wasn't just surviving for the present for the first time. After going through the FFSP process, I discovered that once my expenses were accounted for, I actually had $379 left over each month. This money had been eaten up before in all of the spontaneous outings and unplanned spending I was doing. That dollar amount was huge and powerful for me because it was no longer extra money that got eaten up or lost in the daily spending, but it was my weapon for debt freedom."

At the time of publishing this book, Nechelle's Progress After 18 Months

After a year and a half, Nechelle had:

- Established and completely funded her Life Happens Emergency Fund $2000
- Paid off Credit Card A in 3 months.
- Paid off Credit Card C in 8 months.
- Paid off Credit Card B in 14 months.
- Started saving in her 3-6 Month Emergency Fund

She still had **Credit Card D**, the **Car Loan**,

Student Loan, and **Mortgage** left to pay, but her monthly credit card payments dropped by **$210**, which she now applies toward the next debts and emergency fund.

Updated Debt Status (18 Months In):

Debt	Starting Balance	Current Balance	Status
Credit Card A	$1,200	$0	☐ Paid Off
Credit Card B	$3,000	$0	☐ Paid Off
Credit Card C	$2,500	$0	☐ Paid Off
Credit Card D	$4,200	$2,800	In Progress
Car Loan	$9,500	$6,800	In Progress
Student Loan	$18,000	$16,700	In Progress
Mortgage	$140,000	$138,500	In Progress

Nechelle's Final Reflection

"I may not be debt-free yet, but I've eliminated three credit cards, freed up over $200 in my monthly budget, established my emergency funds, and for the first time in years, I feel like I'm in control. I can see the light at the end of the tunnel. The first time I saw a zero balance on my credit card statement, I cried. It felt like a new chapter was starting — and I wanted to keep turning the pages. The FFSP gave me clarity and a roadmap to my financial future. The snowball plan gave me the speed limit to determine how fast I would get there. Together, they gave me the confidence to know that I can do this. For the first time, I knew exactly where my money was going and how long it would take to get free. Instead of drifting, I had a plan that matched my story, my goals, and my future.

Your Progress Tracker Your Debt Snapshot

Write out your debts below, smallest to largest balance:

Debt Name	Balance	Interest Rate	Min. Payment	Status

My First Target Debt:____________________________
Extra Payment Amount I'll Add: __________________

Progress Wins

___ Debt I Paid Off #1: _________________________
(Date: / /)
___Debt I Paid Off #2: _________________________
(Date: / /)
___Debt I Paid Off #3: _________________________
(Date: / /)

Dr. Juanita's Word of Truth Talk: You Are Not What You Owe

Debt freedom is a journey, and **partial victories are still victories**.
Clearing even one or two accounts reduces your stress, frees up monthly cash flow, and builds momentum toward your bigger goals.

- Each debt you pay off is a **pay raise to your future self**.
- Momentum is just as valuable as math — use both to your advantage.
- Celebrate every step, even before the finish line.

Debt may be part of your story, but it is NOT your identity.

You are a woman of wisdom. You are a woman of strategy. And with a plan, support, and consistency — **you will be debt-free.**

Proverbs 22:7 states, *"The rich rule over the poor, and the borrower is slave to the lender."* NIV

Yes, this verse is real. As I worked through my debt journey, my debt dictated that I show up to work, how long I needed to work, and how many patients I needed to see for the day. You owe yourself freedom. You owe yourself future peace. And that's what we're working toward: one payment at a time. Even if it takes months or years… It's possible. And you don't have to do it alone.

Progress requires pruning. You must release what

no longer serves your next level. When you lighten your load, you accelerate your journey.

Elevation requires release. Letting go isn't weakness-it's wisdom. Every burden you drop gives you space to rise. You don't have to carry it all to move forward. I encourage you to take a powerful look at what needs to be released in your life, financially, emotionally, and spiritually. You'll discover how to eliminate draining habits, reduce debt, and break free from toxic cycles that keep you small and have a negative banking balance and little cash flow. It's time to clear the clutter, rewrite your debt story, and claim the space you were meant to rise into. It's time to move to abundance and peace.

As you eliminate what's been weighing you down, watch how light your journey becomes. Release the guilt, release the debt, and release the pressure. You were made to soar. Now ASCEND.

Your Affirmation

"Debt does not define me. I release every weight that has held me back, and I rise with strategy, strength, and faith. I am free to elevate above limitations and step boldly into abundance." (Anchored in Hebrews 12:1)

Reflection Questions:

1. What financial habits or obligations are holding you back?

2. What are you ready to let go of so you can rise higher?

3. How will your life feel once you're no longer weighed down?

Transformational Testimony

Monique T. — From Paycheck to Peace

Starting Situation:

- Income: $3,400/month (Social Worker, single)
- Living paycheck to paycheck with no savings buffer
- Overdrafted at least twice a month
- Car loan is behind by 1 month, relying on credit cards for groceries
- Avoided opening mail and checking bank accounts

Breakthrough Moment:
During the "Mindset Makeover" module, Monique realized she had equated budgeting with restriction due to childhood experiences of lack. She identified her "WHY" — to create financial stability for her son — and finally felt empowered rather than ashamed.

Transformation:

- Built a starter emergency fund of $600 within 6 weeks
- Used FFSP (Financial Freedom Spending Plan) to gain control over cash flow

- Paid off overdraft and caught up on car loan
- Reduced monthly stress and anxiety, reported sleeping better, and feeling emotionally lighter

Let's go deeper together and Rewrite Your Money Story and Reclaim Your Power. Join the ASCEND Coaching Program

Chapter 5
Nurture and Navigate Your Financial Systems

Be sure you know the condition of your flocks, give careful attention to your herds; for riches do not endure forever, and a crown is not secure for all generations. –Proverbs 27:23-24

"The wise store up choice food and olive oil, but fools gulp theirs down." — Proverbs 21:20

When I finally paused long enough to look at the systems I had in place, or rather, the lack of them, I realized something important: I wasn't managing my business and my personal finances with excellence. I was taking for granted the money that I was bringing in and thinking that it was unending. I had never really been taught how to nurture my money. I knew how to make it, but I hadn't learned how to sustain it, grow it, and protect it.

Maybe that sounds familiar. Maybe you've been showing up for everyone else, working hard, building things that matter, but behind the scenes, your financial systems are fragile, or even nonexistent. You may not feel confident when it comes to credit, savings, or long-term planning-not because you aren't capable, but because no one ever taught you how to steward your finances with intention.

What would shift if you treated your finances like something worth nurturing? What could change if you learned how to navigate the systems designed to work for you, not against you?

Taking the mystery out of managing money with wisdom teaches you how to track your net worth, strengthen your credit, and design systems that support your goals. We're not just managing money-we're nurturing it for growth, accomplishing dreams and destinies, and generational impact.

Understanding Your Financial Framework

Your financial life is made up of systems: credit, banking, benefits, automation, and more. When you understand these systems, you move from reacting to money to mastering it.

Many women feel overwhelmed by financial topics because they've never been taught how these systems work. But here's the truth: you don't need to be an expert—you just need a roadmap. When you know your systems, you can align them with your values and goals. You're no longer operating in confusion—you're leading with clarity and authority.

Navigate Towards Your Future

Building Financial Rhythms and Rituals

Financial nurturing isn't just about budgeting—it's about creating a consistent, meaningful relationship with your money. Just like you water plants or schedule time for your wellness, your finances thrive when they're cared for regularly. That's why establishing financial rhythms and rituals is essential. These habits help you stay in tune with your goals and prevent the drift that happens when life gets busy.

A financial rhythm is a pattern—weekly, bi-weekly, or monthly—where you check in on your money. This could look like a Money Monday routine, where you review spending, transfer savings, and pay bills. Or it might be a monthly Budget and Bless Session, where you revise your budget, assess progress toward your goals, and make room for giving or unexpected expenses. These touch points help you stay proactive instead of reactive.

Financial rituals add meaning and momentum to your journey. Maybe you light a candle, journal your intentions, or pray before making money decisions. Maybe you and your spouse sit down together with your coffee to review the month. These practices create a sense of care and mindfulness, transforming money from a stressor to a stewardship tool.

When you commit to these rhythms, you begin to notice changes—not just in your numbers, but in your confidence. Your spending becomes more intentional, your goals stay visible, and your decisions feel more grounded. These small actions compound over time, leading to peace, clarity, and forward motion.

Understanding Credit Scores and Credit Systems

Your credit score is not a measure of your worth—but it does influence your financial options. It affects everything from loan approvals to interest rates and even insurance premiums.

This section walks you through what's in your credit report, how your score is calculated, and what steps you can take to improve or protect it.

You'll also learn how to access your free credit reports, dispute errors, and understand the five key factors that impact your score (payment history, utilization, length of credit, types of credit, and new inquiries).

With this knowledge, you'll no longer fear your credit—you'll manage it confidently, using it as a tool instead of a trap.

Credit is one of the most misunderstood areas of personal finance, yet it plays a major role in access—access to homes, cars, business funding, and more. Understanding how credit works empowers you to build it intentionally and repair it strategically. Your credit score is not your worth—it's simply a number based on your financial behavior.

Credit scores are calculated based on five main factors: payment history, amounts owed (utilization), length of credit history, types of credit, and new inquiries. The most important? Payment history. Paying on time—even the minimum—shows lenders you're trustworthy. The second most important is utilization—how much of your available credit you're using. Staying under 30% usage keeps your score healthier.

You also want to keep older accounts open (to boost your history length), mix your credit types over time (installment vs. revolving), and avoid too many hard inquiries at once. Understanding these simple rules helps you take control of your credit, rather than fearing it.

Monitoring your credit regularly, disputing inaccuracies, and being strategic with usage allows you to build a strong foundation for bigger financial moves. Good credit isn't about borrowing recklessly—it's about positioning yourself wisely.

Your credit is your **financial trust score**. It determines what you pay for cars, homes, loans, insurance, and sometimes even your job offers.

Know This:

- You are entitled to 1 free credit report from all three bureaus every year
- Your **credit score** ranges between 300–850
- Factors that affect it:
    - Payment history
    - Utilization (credit used vs. credit available)
    - Length of history
    - Types of credit

   - New credit/inquiries

Awareness brings authority.

Banking with Purpose and Intention

Every bank account should have a job. Your accounts should be set up to reflect your real-life needs, reduce untimely decision-making or decision fatigue, and protect your financial boundaries. They should reflect your values and goals. Bank accounts are tools to use to help your money work for you, not against you.

Consider having a banking system such as this one:

- **1 Checking Account** with a connected Savings Account for fixed expenses, including you as a bill; the Savings Account is allocated for Life Happens Emergency Fund. You should be allocating more than your total amount of fixed expenses into this account so that you build an emergency fund over time. For example, if your monthly fixed expenses total $1000. Then you should factor in $1020 -$1050 so that the excess $20-$50 can be used to build your Life Happens Fund and replenish it when you have to withdraw from it.

- **1 Checking Account** with a connected Savings Account for variable expenses and daily spending. Savings Account for overflow amount to help with spending exceeding the allotted amount for the month, so that you don't have to go into your fixed account or other savings accounts that are designated for purposeful purchases. You should also set this account up so that more is deposited into it to allow for the unexpected, and when purchases exceed what has been allotted for. For example, you have allocated $600 for your variable spending. You set it up so that you have $620-$650 going into the account. The extra $20-$50 goes into the savings account to build your overflow to help cover any unexpected spending.

- **3-5 Savings Accounts** for Savings buckets (3-6 Month Emergency Fund, "You" Fund (a savings dedicated to saving for you, Debt Reduction, Short/ Long-Term Savings, Dream Fund)

This creates clarity and makes it easier to manage your financial flow without constantly second-guessing. This also allows you to make sure your expenses are covered for the month and lets you make smarter decisions about spending money that you should not be spending.

Automation supports your system by removing willpower from the equation. When you schedule transfers to savings, automatic bill payments, or recurring debt payments, you ensure consistency even when life is hectic. Automation is self-care—it helps protect your peace while building financial momentum. And when you have allocated the dollar amounts based upon your Financial Freedom Spending Plan, you know what dollar amounts should be going into each account.

You should also use your bank's online tools to track expenses, receive alerts, and avoid overdraft fees. When you send the appropriate dollar amount that is allocated for your expenses, there is no longer a surprise as to whether the money is available. You know how much is needed for each expense now and are able to plan accordingly. Choosing a bank that aligns with your values and offers transparency is another form of empowerment. Your accounts should work for you, not confuse or penalize you.

Tracking and Growing Your Net Worth

> **Net Worth — Your Financial Snapshot**
>
> **Net Worth = Assets – Liabilities**

Your net worth is one of the most powerful measurements of your financial health because it gives the clearest snapshot of your financial reality. It's not just about your income but it's the difference between what you own and what you owe. Assets include things you own—cash, investments, real estate equity, and retirement accounts. Liabilities include what you owe—credit cards, student loans, mortgages, etc. It doesn't matter where you start. What matters is that you begin tracking it.

Revisit this number quarterly. It will show you progress even when your income stays the same. Your net worth shows growth, debt reduction, and wealth accumulation over time. Knowing where you stand helps you know where to go next. This is financial empowerment.

Tracking your net worth helps you see the full picture. You may be making progress even if your day-to-day doesn't feel like it. For example, paying down debt increases your net worth. Growing your savings does too. Watching this number rise over time is deeply encouraging.

It also shifts your mindset from consumer to wealth builder. Instead of just focusing on income and expenses, you start asking: 'How do I grow what I keep?' You begin to prioritize assets, reduce unnecessary debt, and make decisions with long-term impact.

You don't need a six-figure income to build net worth. You need strategy, consistency, and clarity.

It is also very empowering to focus on net worth versus just savings. Because really, if you think about it, the money you save may or may not be yours to keep, especially if you have certain debts. If you default on some of your debts, it can require you to use your savings to pay those off. Therefore, if you consider building your net worth, you think of both sides of the equation. Not just savings, but eliminating debt. Both are items that increase your net worth.

Activate Your Savings Plan

The Emotional Block Around Saving

Saving money is one of the most empowering habits you can build, yet for many women, it feels impossible. That's because saving isn't just about numbers—it's emotional. It stirs up beliefs about scarcity, fear of lack, and the idea that you'll never have enough to get ahead.

This section helps you confront those internal barriers. What do you believe about saving? Do you see it as a punishment or as protection? Do you believe you're capable of creating a cushion for your future?

The truth is, saving is not about having more money—it's about having more vision. It's about believing that your future deserves preparation, even if all you can start with is $10 a month.

Once you release the emotional blocks, saving becomes an act of power. It becomes a declaration that you are not just surviving anymore, you are preparing for peace, opportunity, and abundance.

Why Is Saving So Hard?

For many women, saving money feels like an afterthought. It's that thing we'll "get around to" when the bills are paid… when we have more left over… when life stops being so unpredictable.

But the truth is this: saving is not what you do with extra money — it's what you do with vision and intention. Saving is the "difference maker" sometimes in your dreams, happening, and them not happening. It is also the vehicle to financial freedom, peace, and abundance. If you spend all that you make, you do a disservice to you, the future you, and your family.

Many individuals believe that they earn the right to do with their money what they want whenever they want and feel. The truth of the matter is that it is true, but it is how you do that. There should be a strategic way of doing what you want with the money you earn, and it involves taking into consideration your values, dreams, and goals. It should also take into consideration the unexpected things in life that you have no control over. There is always going to be a rainy day in one season or another, and you should factor it raining at some point in your life. Don't get caught without an umbrella.

Saving should not be about how much you save — it should be about the habit you build in the process. And when you build that habit, even small amounts grow into something powerful.

Why You Need More Than One Savings Account

All savings are not the same, and treating them that way can cause confusion and sabotage your goals. That's why you need more than one savings account, each with its own purpose and label. I refer to these multiple savings accounts as savings buckets.

I recommend five savings buckets: Debt Reduction, Emergency Funds (for unexpected life events, 3-6 month fund), "You" Fund (A savings account dedicated to you). This is included as one of your fixed expense items to make sure you pay yourself. You work for the money. It is a shame that you are the last to be paid. We are changing that system NOW. You are as important as your mortgage, rent, or car payment. Short-Term Fund (for planned expenses like car repairs, birthdays, or travel), and Dream Fund (for investments, big goals, or freedom purchases), and Long-term savings (retirement, financial freedom, abundance, and prosperity).

With savings buckets, you are factored into the

equation of savings by using the "you" savings fund. It's no longer saving for yourself after you have paid all your bills and unplanned spending. This system makes you a bill, and you are treated as such. You work for the money. It is a shame that you are the last to be paid. We are changing that system NOW. You are as important as your mortgage, rent, or car payment. You are one of the fixed expenses that you set up in your Financial Freedom Spending Plan in Chapter 3.

By separating your money into categories, you remove the guilt of spending from the wrong account and reduce the temptation to touch your emergency savings when you want to book a vacation. This system adds structure, removes ambiguity, and makes your savings goals feel real. Each bucket represents a layer of protection and a step toward financial wholeness.

The 5 Bucket Savings Strategy

Let's keep it powerful. You need more than one savings bucket because life has more than one need.

1. Emergency Funds

Life Happens Fund

- Goal: $1000–$2,000 to start
- Purpose: Covers the unexpected — car repairs, medical, home repairs, etc.
- Why it matters: Prevents you from falling back into debt when life happens.

2. 3-6 Month Emergency Fund

- Goal: 3–6 months of expenses
- Purpose: Rent increases, insurance, annual costs, loss of job, illness/ death of loved one etc.
- Why it matters: Helps you plan for things you *know* are coming, as well as those unexpected life happenings that force you to be off of work for an extended period.

3. Debt Reduction Fund

Goal: $1000–$2,000 to start

- Purpose: To eliminate debt faster and more strategically
- Why it matters: To allow your money to be used for your benefit and not to continue to build someone else's dream or profit margin.

4. Dream Fund/ You Fund

- Goal: You choose
- Purpose: Business investments, home, Vacations/ Travel
- Why it matters: To be able to live a destiny-driven life.

5. Long-Term Savings

- Goal: You choose
- Purpose: Retirement, generational wealth

- Why it matters: To be able to move towards a life of financial freedom, abundance, and prosperity.

Make It Automatic

You don't need more discipline—you need better systems. When saving is automatic, it doesn't require willpower or perfect timing. It becomes a seamless habit that builds wealth over time.

Go to each of your banking accounts and set up automatic transfers to each of your savings buckets, whether weekly, biweekly, or monthly. Even a small recurring amount builds consistency and momentum. Automation turns good intentions into guaranteed outcomes. You no longer have to remember or justify your decision—your system does the work for you.

The goal is to make saving a rhythm, not a reaction. This small tweak creates big peace over time and supports the belief that you are building something meaningful.

Celebrate Consistency Over Amount

One of the biggest mistakes people make with saving is waiting until they can 'save big.' But the real power is in saving consistently. Small deposits, made regularly, build both your balance and your belief.

It's time to shift your focus from the amount to the habit. Saving $25 every week may not feel exciting at first—but over a year, it adds up to over $1,000. That's proof that consistency compounds. During COVID, studies showed that the average American did not have $1000 saved up. Many of my clients called me and told me that we were experiencing that "rainy day" I had always told them to save for. Some of them were very grateful to have started their savings buckets, and others were feeling the regret of putting off starting their Financial Freedom Spending Plan until a later date.

Build into your financial system a celebratory step that allows you to celebrate every milestone reached—whether it's your first $100 or your first fully funded emergency fund. Make sure your celebration doesn't include spending the money you just saved, but maybe you have an accountability partner you could share your good news with.

Saving Is a Statement of Faith

At its core, saving is more than a financial practice: it's a spiritual one. It's a declaration that you believe in your future, that you expect good things, and that you are preparing for provision. It's not rooted in fear of 'what if,' but in faith that 'when it's needed, it will be there.'

You are saving not just for emergencies, but for opportunities. Not just for setbacks, but for your next season; for the future you. Saving says: I trust that I will have what I need when I need it. Saving is also a statement of what's to come. It says that you are not satisfied with mediocrity, but you want all that you are able to acquire for yourself, and it puts you in the driver's seat. Let every deposit be a declaration of belief. You're not just putting money in an account—you're making room for abundance to flow.

Reflection Questions:

- How much can you **automate** into savings weekly or monthly?
- Do you have separate savings accounts for each goal?
- What small action can you take this week to activate your savings rhythm?
- How does nurturing your finances impact your sense of peace and control?

Dr. Juanita's Word of Truth

Nurturing your finances is a lifelong act of wisdom. Keep learning, keep refining, and keep showing up. This is an act of loving your future self. You're no longer wandering-you're walking in purpose, with confidence and clarity.

To truly prosper, you must tend to your finances like a garden and learn the systems that govern them. It's about empowerment and stepping boldly into financial literacy and awareness. You don't need to be an expert. But you *do* need to be informed. When you know the system, you stop fearing it and feeling defeated by it. You don't need to be a finance major. You just need a roadmap. You don't have to wait until it's "a good time." You just need to decide that **your future is worth funding and** then move on it.

Your Affirmation

"I am a faithful steward of my resources, nurturing them with gratitude and navigating them with intention and wisdom. I know my numbers, I honor my worth, and I grow in peace and prosperity."
(Anchored in Proverbs 27:23–24)

Transformational Spotlight

Alyssa M. — Faith Meets Financial Strategy

Starting Situation:

- Income: $2,800/month (Part-time Church Admin + side speaking)
- $9,000 in credit card debt and no retirement plan
- Believed trusting God meant "He would provide later"
- Didn't budget—felt overwhelmed and relied on prayer alone for breakthroughs

Breakthrough Moment:
In designing the "Prosperity Plan," Alyssa learned that **stewardship and faith go hand in hand**. She realized that faith wasn't about neglecting planning, but about partnering with God intentionally.

Transformation:

- Created a $1,200 savings cushion for emergencies

- Allocated income using the FFSP
- Paid off two credit cards in 4 months
- Began investing $100/month in a Roth IRA

Access Bonus Material from Dr. Juanita

All the resources in this book and those in the Quick Reference Toolbox will help you to formulate new financial habits. Scan the QR to receive bonus material or visit askdrjuanita.com/contact.

Dr. Juanita

Chapter 6

Design and Dominate Your Prosperity Plan

"Write the vision and make it plain on tablets… though it tarry, wait for it; it will surely come."
— Habakkuk 2:2–3

Now it's time to bring it all together-to move from planning to action and from dreaming to doing. It's time to define your personal vision of prosperity, build 6-7 figure foundations, create income streams, and craft your legacy. You can continue to strengthen your confidence, ensuring that what you build will last and reflect your highest values. Prosperity is not accidental; it's intentional.

Defining Your Vision of Prosperity

Prosperity is more than just having money. It's about living a life of peace, purpose, and abundance on your own terms aligned with your highest values. Before you can build a plan, you must define what prosperity truly looks and feels like for you.

Too often, women are taught to pursue society's version of success: a big house, a fancy car, designer clothes, and status. But true prosperity is deeply personal. For me, it's the ability to live with freedom and abundance, give generously, rest peacefully, and thrive without financial fear.

Take a moment to imagine your most peaceful and prosperous life. Where are you waking up each day? What kind of work are you doing? Who are you spending time with? How are you giving back? What does your schedule look like? These aren't just dreams; they're clues to what you truly value, what brings you peace, and where your financial goals should be rooted.

Defining your prosperity vision allows you to create financial goals that are not only ambitious but aligned. It gives you a measuring stick that goes beyond money. For some, prosperity means financial independence and early retirement. For others, it means paying off a home, starting a nonprofit organization, traveling the world, or simply never stressing over bills again. Maybe it's debt freedom, or time with family, or giving generously, or living simply but securely.

When you define what prosperity looks like in your life, you can stop comparing yourself to others and start chasing what matters most to you. Your vision is your compass. It helps you say yes to the right opportunities and no to the distractions. It centers your goals with purpose. Without a clear vision, it's easy to feel aimless or overwhelmed, working hard but not feeling fulfilled. But with a defined vision of prosperity, every small financial decision becomes a brick laid toward your dream life.

You now have permission to release society's definition and replace it with your own, one that honors your season, faith, and dreams. Here is where wealth becomes personal. And when it's personal, it becomes powerful.

The Three Levels of Prosperity

From Provision to Peace to Purpose

Level 1: Provision – *"I Have What I Need"*

This is the foundation.
At this level, prosperity means your basic needs are met consistently and without stress. You're no longer living paycheck to paycheck, and you're able to handle emergencies without panic.

What it looks like:

- Consistent income and a working budget
- Emergency fund started
- Debt under control or being eliminated
- Basic savings habits are in place

Reflection Prompt:
Where in my life has God already provided for me? What does "enough" look like for me right now?

Level 2: Peace – *"I'm Not Just Covered — I'm Calm"*

This is emotional prosperity.
Peace comes when your finances no longer keep you up at night. You feel safe, secure, and in control of your money. You've established rhythm, margin, and breathing room.

What it looks like:

- Zero fear of checking your accounts
- Margin in your monthly finances
- Emotional freedom from shame or guilt about money
- Systems in place: automation, tracking, planning

Reflection Prompt:
What practices can I put in place to protect my peace financially?

Level 3: Purpose – *"I'm Building Beyond Myself"*

This is legacy-level prosperity.
You're not just sustaining yourself — you're building for generations, giving generously, and aligning your money with your mission. This level activates *overflow*.

What it looks like:

- 6-figure bank account or wealth-building in motion
- Giving without fear (tithes, offerings, causes)
- Supporting dreams, funding others
- Financial freedom that fuels life's calling

Reflection Prompt:
How does my money align with my life's purpose? Who am I called to bless with my overflow?

The **Ladder View** of the 3 Levels of Prosperity — visually climbing from **Provision** to **Peace** to **Purpose**.

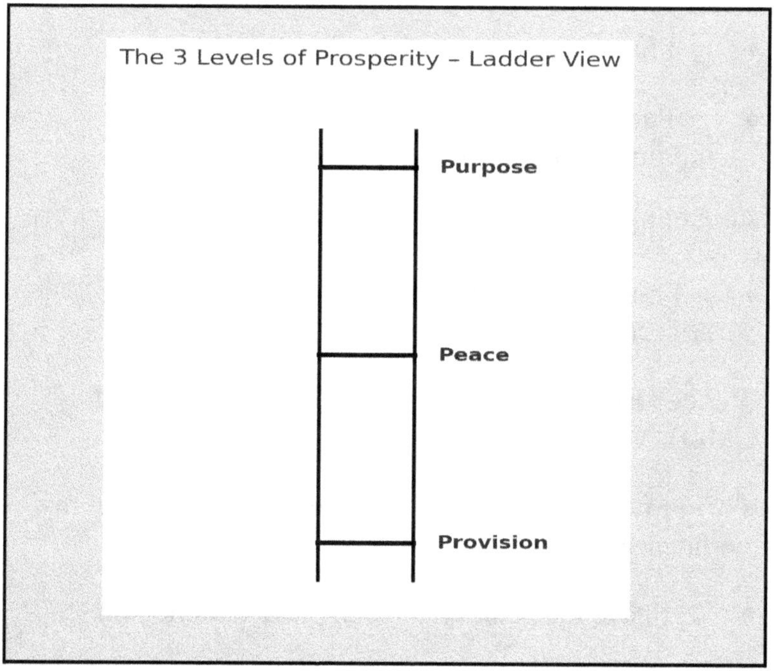

Prosperity Ladder Levels Assessment Tool

This self-assessment helps you identify which level of prosperity you're currently operating in — Provision, Peace, or Purpose — and where you're being called to climb next.

How to Use This Tool:

Read each statement below and score yourself from 1 (Not true at all) to 5 (Completely true). Tally your total score for each level to determine your current stage of prosperity.

Provision (Essentials: I Have What I Need)

- __ I am able to pay my bills on time each month. (1–5)
- __ I have a working monthly budget. (1–5)
- __ I am actively working to reduce debt or have minimal debt. (1–5)
- __ I have at least one month of expenses saved. (1–5)
- __I rarely feel panic when unexpected expenses arise. (1–5)

Peace (Emotional Security: I'm Covered and Calm)

- __ I feel emotionally secure when thinking about my finances. (1–5)
- __ I have financial systems in place (automation,

tracking, saving). (1–5)

- __I do not argue or stress often about money. (1–5)
- __ I enjoy looking at my bank account without anxiety. (1–5)
- __ I feel peace knowing I'm on a financial path with margin. (1–5)

Purpose (Overflow and Impact: I'm Building Beyond Me)

- __ I have more than enough and feel ready to bless others. (1–5)
- __I am consistently giving, tithing, or sowing into others. (1–5)
- __ My income allows me to support causes, people, or legacy goals. (1–5)
- __ I'm building wealth to leave an inheritance or long-term impact. (1–5)
- __ I feel deeply aligned with how my money supports my mission. (1–5)

Scoring:

Add the scores for each section. The section with the highest score indicates your current level of prosperity.
Total for Provision: _______
Total for Peace: _______
Total for Purpose: _______

Reflection Prompt:

What level are you currently in? What practical or spiritual steps can help you rise to the next level of prosperity?

The goal is to climb the ladder by raising your level towards Prosperity.

Building 6-Figure Foundations

Many women dream of earning six and seven figures, but few are taught how to build the foundation required to sustain it. Earning more money without structure, clarity, and discipline can lead to even more stress, not less. That's why building a 6-figure income starts with building a 6-figure mindset and system. It's not just about the dollar amount, it's about creating stability, systems, and stewardship that allow that income to grow and last.

Your foundation begins with clarity. What does your ideal income look like? What will it take to reach it through your career, business, or side income? And most importantly, what will you do with that income once it arrives? Without a plan, six figures can disappear just as easily as five. With a plan, six figures can create legacy, freedom, and generational wealth.

Next, you need structure. This means knowing your monthly expenses, allocating your income with intention, automating savings and debt payoff, and separating personal from business finances. Many high earners still live paycheck to paycheck; not because they don't earn enough, but because they haven't built a structure that allows their money to work for them.

Sustainability is key. A 6-figure lifestyle isn't worth it if it costs your peace, purpose, or relationships. Ask yourself: Is my current path to six figures sustainable? Does it honor my values and energy? Your foundation must include boundaries, rest, and a rhythm that supports longevity. That's how you build wealth that doesn't burn you out.

Remember, building six figures isn't just about more, it's about mastery. Mastering your mindset, your systems, and your stewardship is what prepares you to not only earn more, but to keep it, grow it, and enjoy it.

Building Multiple Streams of Income

In today's economy, relying on a single source of income is like walking a financial tightrope. Any disruption can throw your entire life off balance. That's why building multiple streams of income is a foundational principle in your prosperity plan. It's not just about making more money-it's about increasing stability, expanding opportunity, and creating financial flow that frees you from paycheck-to-paycheck living.

Multiple income streams allow you to diversify your earnings so that you're not dependent on one job, one client, or one business. These streams might include earned income (salary or hourly work), side hustle, rental income, dividend-producing investments, digital products, coaching, or consulting. The key is not to chase everything, but to choose streams that align with your skills and interests.

When you build income streams intentionally, you multiply both your income and your impact. Maybe you use your professional expertise to offer freelance services on the side. Or you create a digital course to share what you know. Maybe you invest in real estate, start a weekend business with a friend, or build a product once and sell it passively. Every stream you add builds your financial foundation-and gives you more options. Start where you are. You don't have to launch five streams overnight. Begin with one, then master and expand.

Ask yourself: What can I monetize from what I already know or do? What gaps in the market could I fill? What's a problem I can solve for others that would also create income for me? Every new stream begins with a single idea and a small step.

Legacy Starts Now

Legacy isn't something you leave behind someday after you die; it's something you build while you live with every decision, every dollar, and every intention. Too often, we think of legacy as something reserved for the wealthy or the elderly. But the truth is, your legacy begins the moment you start living on purpose. It's about impact, inheritance, and influence, and how you're using your life and finances to shape the world around you.

Financially, legacy means building assets that will outlive you. This includes savings, investments, real estate, insurance, businesses, and even wisdom passed down through generations. But it also includes your generosity: how you give, serve, mentor, and support others today. Legacy is about positioning your family and community to thrive, not just survive.

Creating a legacy starts with clarity. What do you want to be known for? What values do you want your children, nieces, nephews, or community to carry forward? What do you want your money to accomplish long after you're gone? These questions become the seeds of your legacy plan, one that includes estate planning, life insurance, wills or trusts, and documented instructions for your assets.

But more than anything, legacy is a mindset. It's the choice to build with purpose. Whether you're creating generational wealth, teaching your children about money, starting a family business, or funding scholarships, your legacy is your long-term love letter to the future. You don't need millions to create one. You just need vision, intention, and action.

Your legacy is for the generations who will rise because you chose to ASCEND.

Practicing Confidence

Dominating your prosperity requires confidence. Confidence isn't something you either have or don't have-it's something you practice, grow, and build over time. In your financial journey, confidence is the quiet strength that allows you to make decisions, take action, and trust yourself even when the numbers don't look perfect or the path feels unfamiliar and foggy. Confidence is the companion to prosperity; it keeps you moving forward when doubt tries to pull you back.

Practicing confidence means recognizing that you are capable, even if you've made mistakes in the past. It means giving yourself credit for the progress you've made, and believing that your goals are not just possible, but probable with determination and discipline. Confidence is not arrogance; it's alignment. It's standing firmly in your vision, knowing that you're equipped to handle the process, one step at a time.

Many women were taught to shrink financially; to play small, to avoid risk, or to rely on others for money decisions. Practicing confidence is an act of moving beyond fear. It's choosing to raise your voice in rooms that matter, ask questions without shame, and take leadership over your finances. It's walking into a bank, a negotiation, a business deal, or a budgeting session with boldness and peace.

The more you practice confidence, the more it becomes your default. You begin to trust your instincts, use your resources wisely, and stretch beyond what you thought was possible. Financial confidence is not built on the big wins; it's built in the daily choices. Each time you take control, stay committed, or step out of your comfort zone, your confidence expands.

Putting Your Purpose on Paper

It's time to write the vision and make it plain. This helps you take everything in your heart and translate it into a concrete, prosperous financial plan.

I remember the first time I allowed myself to dream beyond just getting by. I was tired of managing crises, tired of shrinking my desires, tired of working so hard only to feel like I wasn't moving forward. It wasn't that I lacked ambition; I lacked a plan that reflected my vision. I always had a vision of living a prosperous life. But what did that actually mean to me and for me? When I finally put pen to paper and began mapping out what prosperity looked like for me, everything started to shift.

You might be there right now, ready for more, but unsure how to build it. You've stabilized, simplified, cleared out the clutter, started your debt reduction, and taken control of your financial path. Now it's time to design the life you actually want, and walk in it with confidence, clarity, and faith. Your dream doesn't have to stay a dream. It can become a blueprint.

What would your life look like if you built it on your own definition of prosperity? What if it's not about chasing success, but living out the vision God planted in your heart?

Your prosperity plan is crafted from vision mapping your desires, dreams, and goals to identifying multiple streams of income and building a legacy. Your prosperity plan allows you to define what abundance means for you, practice the confidence to walk it out, and dominate your next level with purpose. No more shrinking. It's time to rise.

This is where faith meets action. No more vague wishes. You should design a Prosperity Plan that reflects who you are, where you're going, and how you'll get there.

This is the shift from dreaming to doing, and it's where your future begins to take shape.

Your Prosperity Plan deserves both intention and accountability—and this section gives you the tools for both.

Step 1: Define What Prosperity Means to YOU

Prosperity is intentional. Vision, planning, and bold execution are required. Forget what Instagram, Facebook, or your peers say. This is about YOUR version of abundance; No one else's. Ask yourself**:**

- "What does a prosperous life feel like for me?"
- "What does prosperity look like for me in 1 year / 3 years / 5 years?"
- "What streams of income will I activate?"
- "How much do I want to give, save, and invest monthly?"
- "What does financial peace feel like?"
- "What impact do I want to leave behind?"

Step 2: Set Your 1–3–5 Year Financial Vision

Create SMARTER PATH goals. Let your future self speak through these numbers.

Goal Type	1 Year	3 Year	5 Year
Savings	$________	$________	$________
Debt	$________	$________	$________
Giving	$________	$________	$________
Business/Career	$________	$________	$________
Lifestyle (Home, Travel, etc.)	$________	$________	$________

Step 3: Take Courageous Steps Towards Your Goals

You were created to prosper. Don't shrink your vision. Design boldly, plan intentionally, and dominate your next level with faith and focus. Where your focus is, your actions will go. Your dreams are not random; they're divine assignments.

As you write your vision and take courageous steps toward it, remember that discipline and faith walk hand in hand. Keep building, keep believing, and keep showing up for yourself. You're not just chasing prosperity, but you're creating it; your Prosperity.

Step 4: Set Up Your Accountability Systems

Prosperity doesn't happen in isolation. You must be very purposeful in this process. Create a financial check-in rhythm (weekly/ monthly), a system to track net worth quarterly, and select a coach or mentor for accountability. Put it all in writing. This is not just a wish list—it's a Prosperity Plan.

Do you have:

- A financial check-in rhythm (weekly/monthly)?
- A system to track net worth quarterly?
- A coach, mentor, or partner for accountability?

Put it in writing. This is not just a wish list — it's a **Prosperity Plan.**

Step 5: Revisit Your Financial Freedom Spending Plan

Go back to your FFSP and review to revise to make sure you are taking advantage of your spending categories to reduce any unnecessary spending that you need to. Review your net worth number from Chapter 5 and update it quarterly, and your debt reduction from Chapter 4 monthly. Celebrate every shift, no matter how small. This is your proof that you are building: dollar by dollar, decreasing debt, increasing savings, and a clearer vision and purpose.

Prosperity Plan Journal Prompt

- What does financial freedom look like in my daily life?
- How will I know I'm walking in it?
- What legacy am I building?
- What is my next powerful step?

Step 6: Build your "Six-Figure" Bank Account

I want to normalize something powerful for you: you can have a "six-figure" bank account. And you don't need to make six figures to start building it. I have included my "Six-Figure" Bank Account Blueprint.

The 6-Figure Bank Account Blueprint

"Beloved, I pray that you may prosper in all things and be in health, just as your soul prospers." — 3 John 1:2

While going through my financial journey, I never imagined I'd be writing a section like this: a "Six-Figure Bank Account Blueprint". I felt like I had messed up so badly that I was not going to ever see my money work for me ever again. But let me tell you what I learned along the way: money is very intentional and deliberate. It goes where you tell it to go. And if you don't direct it, it just goes wherever. I just had to make sure that my systems were current and strategic to make my money go where I wanted it to go and to do what I wanted it to do.

So, I began to operate in a consistent way to make sure it did just what I needed and wanted it to do. I didn't know at the time that I would be calling it a blueprint. I created this blueprint because I needed to build my money back up. I had a business to run and a life to live, so I didn't have time for it to go away from me. I didn't know at the time that I would be creating a framework that I would later refer to as the "Six-Figure Bank Account Blueprint".

Along my journey, I learned: Prosperity is not about luck. It's not even just about income. It's about intention, alignment, and strategy. It's about deciding that overflow and abundance belong to you, too. And then create a system that matches your faith and dreams.

Shift Your Mindset: Six Figures is Not a Fantasy

If you've never seen more than a few hundred or a few thousand in your account, six figures might feel out of reach — like trying to grab something behind an invisible wall. But here's your truth: That "wall" is often made of fear, financial trauma, lack of knowledge, and generational patterns — not actual limitations.

Start by declaring this: **"I am a faithful steward of overflow and abundance. I attract, manage, and multiply money and opportunities with purpose and intention."**

Your belief is your bank account's foundation to build upon. Before we even talk numbers, we talk identity. Who do you believe you are when it comes to money?

Break It Down: $100K Isn't One Giant Leap

Have you ever thought about the amount of money that has passed through your hands and bank account in your lifetime? I did! And the number was eye-opening. So, imagine if you keep just a portion of what passes through your account. It might change how you perceive your account moving forward. It changed my perception of my account. It was no longer the account that retained sums of money to pay someone else, but I began to look at it as the account that would fund my **Prosperity**. That shift helped me to direct my funds in a way that would land me more money in my own account for my future and the future me.

Let's do some quick math:

Monthly Savings	Timeline to $100K
$600/month ($300/ check)	13.9 years
$800/month ($400/ check)	10.4 years
$1,000/month ($500/ check)	8.3 years
$2000/month ($1000/ check)	4.1 years

Even if you start small — $100/week, or $20/day — you're on the path. The number feels big until you put it into a plan. Depending on your income, you may be closer to a six-figure bank account than you think. And even if you don't reach six figures, wouldn't it be great to land somewhere close to it.

Prosperity Practice: Map Your Milestone Journey

Use the tracker below to write your monthly savings goal and mark your progress toward $100,000.

$___ / month x ___ months = $100,000

Fill in your target and revisit this each month.

The 3Ps of Building a Six-Figure Bank Account

1. Prioritize Saving:
Treat savings like a non-negotiable bill. Automate it. Even $25 a week adds up.

2. Protect Your Progress:

Avoid lifestyle inflation. As your income increases, so should your *savings*, not just your spending.

3. Prosper with Purpose:
Tie your money to your mission. Give your dollars direction and focus: peace of mind, options, generosity, legacy.

Build your Multiple Income Stream Flow

Freelance Writing or editing; childcare or elderly companion services; laundry, meal prep, or cleaning services; rideshare driving

As we have said before, having multiple streams of income is critical to building prosperity. You can visit the toolbox for a detailed list of income stream options.

"Prosper Like a Pro" Habits List

Prosperous people have rituals and rhythms that they do daily and/ or weekly. You don't find them just waiting around for life to give them something. They are consistently making moves and happenings on a regular basis that promote financial and emotional prosperity. Some examples of these habits include:

- Weekly money dates
- Morning prosperity declarations
- Investing 10 minutes in your financial system or prosperity plan daily or weekly
- Using a "Prosperity Jar" to collect change, bills, or blessings

- Avoiding comparison and tracking your own growth regularly

Six-Figure Financial Identity Affirmations and Prayer

Say these aloud daily or during your money date each week:

i. "Prosperity is my birthright and responsibility."
ii. "I am wealthy in wisdom, purpose, and overflow."
iii. "I am not afraid to hold large amounts of money."
iv. "My bank account grows as my vision expands."
v. "I am a lender and not a borrower."
vi. "I deserve a peaceful, plentiful financial life."
vii. "I am ready for six-figure stewardship."

Closing Prayer

"Heavenly Father, I thank You that You are my source and my provider. You said that I would be mighty in the land, and I thank you today. You promised that if I honor You with my resources, You will open the windows of heaven and pour out blessings I cannot contain (Malachi 3:10). I declare that goodness and mercy follow me, and blessings are overtaking me as I walk in Your ways (Deuteronomy 28:2).

Make me a wise steward, Lord, that I may lend and not borrow, build and not break, give and not withhold. Establish the work of my hands, enlarge my territory, and let abundance flow through me to be a blessing to others. Today, I choose overflow not just for me, but for the legacy I will leave, the peace I will carry, and the people I will empower. I trust You to give me the desires of my

heart as I delight myself in You (Psalm 37:4).
In Jesus' name, Amen."

Reflection Prompt:

What would having $100,000 saved mean to you — emotionally, spiritually, and financially?
What would it allow you to do, give, experience, or finally lay down? Take time here. Write it out. See it. Believe it. Let this be the moment you no longer question if you're *worthy* of overflow and abundance.

Dr. Juanita's Word of Truth

Prosperity Is More Than Wealth — It's Wellness + Purpose + Peace!

True prosperity isn't just a number in the bank. It's **clarity**, **peace**, **impact**, and **alignment** with the life you're meant to live. Here you are designing a financial future that feels and looks like freedom and abundance. No more random goals. No more reactionary living. This is where your values become a vision, and your vision becomes a plan. This journey isn't about perfection; it's about progression, being better today than when you started this book.

You've aligned your mindset. You've clarified your goals. You've faced your numbers. You've built stability and strength through savings, tackling debt, and creating systems. Now, you lead with purpose. You are not just rising. You are rewriting your money story and rebuilding the future for yourself, your family, and generations to come.

This is your Prosperity Plan. And this is just the beginning.

You are ASCENDing!!!

Your Affirmation

"I design a life of purpose, prosperity, and legacy. My vision is clear, my plan is strong, and my steps are ordered. I walk in faith, strategy, and dominion — creating wealth that outlives me."
(Anchored in Habakkuk 2:2–3)

Transformation Spotlights:

Jasmine--from Limiting Lies to Growing Net Worth

"Dr. Juanita, I make decent money, but I never feel like I have anything to show for it. I'm tired of being on the hamster wheel. I have debt that feels like it's never going away, and I don't even know where my money goes each month. I feel ashamed because I should know better, but I don't. I just want peace. I want to feel in control of my money instead of my money controlling me. I don't feel like I will ever get ahead."

When Jasmine first entered the ASCEND Coaching Program, she was overwhelmed by debt, juggling bills, and unsure of where her money was going each month.

Like so many high-achieving women, she was successful on the outside, but carrying silent financial stress on the inside.

Over time, Jasmine faithfully walked through the ASCEND framework:

- **Awaken & Align** – She uncovered limiting beliefs like *"I'll never get ahead"* and replaced them with truth: *"I am a wise steward, and I am capable of building wealth."*

- **Stabilize & Strengthen** – She created her first true budget, set up automatic bill pay, and built consistency with tithing and saving.

- **Control & Clarify** – She tracked every dollar and built a zero-based "Peace Budget." In the process, she found $600 per month in overspending and redirected it toward her goals.

- **Eliminate & Elevate** – Using a hybrid of the Snowball and Avalanche methods, she paid off $12,500 in credit cards and personal loans in just 18 months, saving thousands in interest.

- **Nurture & Navigate** – Jasmine improved her credit score by over 100 points, opened three labeled savings accounts (Emergency, Short-Term, and Dream Fund), and now tracks her net worth quarterly.

Now, Jasmine is in the **Design & Dominate stage** of her Prosperity Plan. She has:

- **$8,000 in her Emergency Fund** (3 months of

expenses covered)

- **$5,000 in her Short-Term Fund** for upcoming travel and annual expenses
- **$2,500 in her Dream Fund** she's building toward her first investment property
- A debt-free lifestyle — she uses credit wisely but never carries balances
- A credit score of **740** that opens doors to better financial opportunities

Most importantly, Jasmine is learning that prosperity isn't just about money; it's about stewardship, impact, and purpose.

She now has a 1–3–5 Year Prosperity Vision:

- **1 Year:** Max out her Roth IRA contributions and grow her Dream Fund to $10,000
- **3 Years:** Purchase her first investment property and grow her net worth by $50,000
- **5 Years:** Launch a scholarship fund to help young women pursue higher education

Her Prosperity Plan isn't just numbers on a page; it's a lifestyle of peace, stewardship, and impact.

Latasha: Rise to Peace & Prosperity

"I always thought making more money would fix everything. But I had income — I didn't have clarity,

peace, or a plan."

Latasha is a 38-year-old healthcare professional earning well over $90k per year — but with no savings, rising debt, and a gnawing sense of shame around her money decisions. On paper, she was "doing well." She had a solid job, her own apartment, and was the one in her family whom others leaned on for help. But her reality told a different story. It was filled with financial anxiety, late-night online shopping, and zero savings.

Every time she got a bonus, tax refund, or raise, it was gone before she could build momentum. Her checking account hovered around $200 at month's end, and the emotional weight of "should be further by now" began to take its toll. There was always something that pulled her two steps back: car repairs, family needs, retail therapy.

When she joined the ASCEND coaching program, she admitted: *"I feel broken because I know better, but I'm not doing better. I always thought making more money would fix everything. But I had income, I just wasn't managing it well. I was exhausted. Not just physically, but all of the above: financially, emotionally, spiritually. My money had no real direction. And neither did I."*

Through the program, Latasha faced her money story and is rewriting it with grace. She created her Financial Freedom Spending Plan and is using it as the first form of budgeting in her adult life. She has also automatized her finances and saved her first $10K in 7 months. Latasha has begun to tithe with confidence and has shifted from financial survival to intentional prosperity. Today, she's still earning her income, but now, every dollar has a direction. Her savings is growing, her peace is back, and her purpose is clear.

"Now, when I look at my account, I don't see just money. I see margin, mission, and momentum. If I can do this, so can you. I used to feel like money was always slipping through my fingers, and now I feel in control and at peace. The ASCEND framework didn't just change my finances; it changed the way I see myself. Don't be afraid to start where you are. Every step forward is proof that you're rising."

When Latasha joined the ASCEND coaching program, she didn't know what to expect. She thought she'd learn some budgeting tips. Instead, she got a financial awakening.

Through her Financial Freedom Spending Plan and Prosperity Plan, Latasha learned that peace wasn't about how much she made. It was about how she managed, multiplied, and moved her money with purpose.

She started asking the right questions: what do I *want* my money to do, where is my money going without my permission, and what is the cost of continuing the same patterns? Latasha set a bold but clear goal: $100,000 in her bank account within 36 months.

Here's how she's making it happen:

1. Income Awareness & Automation

- Created a Financial Freedom Spending Plan, zero-based, and automated her bills and savings.

- Redirected $1,200/month to savings ($600 from cutting spending, $600 from side income).
- Opened a high-yield savings account and a money market account for overflow.

2. Intentional Side Hustles

- Picked up 2 extra shifts/month at her clinic (approx. $600/month).
- Started a side business offering coaching services: a passion aligned with her career.
- Sold gently-used clothes, electronics, and furniture online, using the profits to fund her "$100K account."

3. Monthly Milestone Goals

She broke the $100K goal into achievable steps:

- Year 1: Save $20K
- Year 2: Save an additional $35K
- Year 3: Complete with a $45K final stretch

"Before ASCEND, I thought six figures in a bank account was something rich people had. Now I see it's what aligned women can have: women with a plan, peace, and a purpose. I still make the same money, but I'm not the same woman."

At the time of writing this book, Latasha saved $9,400 in her first 7 months, paid off a lingering $3,000 credit card debt, decluttered her home and her finances, and gained confidence to say "no" to overspending and "yes" to overflow.

Latasha's story proves that you don't have to earn a million to save six figures. What you need is intention, dedication, discipline, a system, and the belief that overflow belongs to you, too.

Dr. Juanita: From Silent Stress and Strain to Stability and Strength

When I look back on my financial journey, I see the evidence of God's grace and the power of clarity. There was a time when I carried the weight of hundreds of thousands of dollars in business and personal debt.

Through the same ASCEND framework I now teach, I rebuilt my life:

- **Awaken & Align** – I faced the shame and guilt I carried about money and began replacing lies with truth. I spoke scripture over my finances and affirmed: *"I am not what I owe; I am who God says I am."*

- **Stabilize & Strengthen** – I created systems for my personal and business finances, putting structure where there had been chaos.

- **Control & Clarify** – I tracked every dollar coming in and out. I built my first true FFSP, and for the first time, I could see clearly.

- **Eliminate & Elevate** – I strategically paid off **over $700,000 in debt** across business loans, credit lines, and personal obligations, using a mixture of Snowball and Avalanche Debt Reduction methods. Each payoff gave me back both dollars and peace of mind.

- **Nurture & Navigate** – I rebuilt my savings, restored my credit, and began tracking my net worth regularly. The numbers weren't perfect at first, but they told a story of progress instead of panic.

Now, in the **Design & Dominate stage**, I am living my Prosperity Plan:

- I maintain fully funded **emergency reserves** for both my personal life and my business.
- I steward my resources with systems that give me clarity and freedom.
- I am building a **legacy plan**, focused on multiple streams of income, generational wealth, and creating impact far beyond myself.
- Most importantly, I live with the peace that comes from knowing I no longer serve money — money serves the purpose God gave me.

My Prosperity Plan is about me designing and living the life that allows me the freedom, peace, and abundance. It's no longer just about survival but about stability and strength. It's about impact. It's about legacy. It's about showing other women that if I could rise from debt, shame, and chaos to clarity and freedom, **they can too**.

Designing your Prosperity Plan is not about "arriving." It's about creating alignment between your money and your mission. Like Jasmine, Latasha, and myself, you may begin with paying off debt and building savings, but "ASCENDing" means designing a life where prosperity flows through you — for yourself, your family, and your legacy.

"I know what it feels like to be buried under debt, overwhelmed by responsibility, and silently wondering if freedom is even possible. I also know what it feels like to come out on the other side — with clarity, peace, and purpose. If God could take my financial mess and turn it into a message, He can do the same for you. You are not behind. You are not too far gone. You are "ASCENDing".

ASCEND
from Paycheck to Prosperity
FREE
Toolkit
Dr. Juanita Taylor

Chapter 7

"ASCENDing": Living Your Prosperity Plan (Conclusion)

"Your story doesn't end in survival. You're "ASCENDing" now."

What "ASCENDing" Looks Like

"ASCENDing" isn't just about being "good with money."
It's about walking in a new financial identity — one where peace replaces panic, and purpose drives every decision.

When you are "ASCENDing":

- You make decisions from clarity, not fear.
- You know exactly where your money is going — in your personal life and your business.
- You are debt-free, or your remaining debts are moving steadily toward zero with a proven plan.
- You save with consistency, not as an afterthought.
- You have multiple systems — from automated bill pay to a net worth tracker — working in the background so you can focus on life, not just money.

- Your prosperity plan is not a dream on paper — it's active, measurable, and unfolding before your eyes.

Vision Snapshot

Imagine waking up on a Monday morning without a pit in your stomach about bills or business cash flow.
Your accounts are balanced.
Your savings are growing every month.
Your debts are shrinking without you feeling deprived.
Your business is profitable and positioned for growth.
Your giving is consistent, joyful, and impactful.
Your money now serves you and the life God called you to live.

Mini Spotlights — Women Who Are "ASCENDing"

Tasha – Paid off $14,000 in personal debt in 10 months, increased her credit score 92 points, and now funds her retirement account with confidence.

Maribel – Stabilized her business finances, eliminated $5,000 in vendor debt, and built a 3-month business reserve fund that keeps her payroll stress-free.

Danielle – Reduced her combined personal and business debt by $18,700, grew savings by $8,500, and improved her net worth by $18,500 in one year.

Angela – Gained the courage to raise her rates, freeing up $1,200/month that now goes directly into her Dream

Fund for a future property purchase.

Measurable Wins of "ASCENDing"

From the women who have embraced the ASCEND framework:

- **Debt Freedom** – An average of $10,000–$25,000 in debt eliminated in the first 12–18 months.
- **Savings Growth** – Emergency funds built from zero to $5,000+ in under a year.
- **Credit Score Gains** – 50–100+ point increases after implementing Navigate Financial Systems strategies.
- **Net Worth Increases** – A shift from negative net worth to positive, often by $15,000–$30,000 in the first year.
- **Confidence & Peace** – The priceless result of knowing you have a plan that works.

Your Next Step

You've walked through every pillar of ASCEND:

- Awaken & Align Your Mindset
- Stabilize & Strengthen Your Finances
- Control & Clarify Your Cash Flow
- Eliminate & Elevate Your Finances
- Nurture & Navigate Financial Systems

- Design & Dominate in Your Prosperity Plan

Now, it's time to live them, not as theory, but as practice.
Here's how to keep ASCENDing:

1. **Review Quarterly** – Update your net worth, review your prosperity plan, and recalibrate your goals.

2. **Automate Your Wins** – Keep bills, savings, and investments on autopilot.

3. **Stay Accountable** – Whether it's a coach, mentor, or peer group, stay in the community.

4. **Celebrate Milestones** – Debt paid off? Savings milestone hit? Mark it. Celebrate it.

The Prosperity Declaration

I am a wise steward of the resources God has entrusted to me (Luke 16:10).

The windows of heaven are open over my life, pouring out a blessing so great I will not have room enough to receive it (Malachi 3:10).

Blessings are overtaking me because I walk in obedience to the Word (Deuteronomy 28:2).

I am the lender and not the borrower, the head and not the tail, above only and not beneath (Deuteronomy 28:12-13).

The Lord gives me the desires of my heart as I delight in Him (Psalm 37:4).

I walk in clarity, confidence, and peace in my finances.

I honor my values with every financial decision I make.

I eliminate what no longer serves my purpose and build what creates freedom for myself, my family, and generations to come.

My money is a tool, not my master.

I am ASCENDing - and I will continue to rise, leaving a legacy of faith, freedom, and abundance.

Dr. Juanita's Final Word of Truth

This is not the end — it's the launch point.
Your financial freedom is no longer a "someday" wish. You've built the mindset, the systems, and the plan. Now, take these tools and rise into the life you were meant to live — fully funded, fully free, and fully aligned.

You are "ASCENDing". And this is just the beginning.

Conclusion: The Journey Continues

As you've walked through each section of this book, from awakening to designing your prosperity plan, you've taken powerful steps toward rewriting your financial story. You've faced truths, shifted beliefs, built systems, and defined what true wealth means for you.

But remember, this is not the end; it's a new beginning. Financial freedom is a journey, not a destination. There will be moments of triumph and moments of tension, but with every decision, you are rising higher.

Continue to review, revise, and revisit your vision regularly. Stay rooted in your purpose, remain aligned with your values, and surround yourself with tools, people, and systems that support your growth.

Your legacy is being written in real time. Keep ascending. You were never meant to just survive; you were created to thrive. Let this book be your foundation and your launching pad. Prosperity is not just possible; it's already in motion.

Keep ASCENDing!!!

Your Affirmation: I Am ASCENDing

I am not my past — I am God's promise.
I walk in wisdom, stewardship, and peace.
I release shame and rise in strength.
The windows of heaven are open over me, pouring out blessings I cannot contain (Malachi 3:10).
I am the lender and not the borrower, above only and not beneath (Deuteronomy 28:12–13).
I delight myself in the Lord, and He gives me the desires of my heart (Psalm 37:4).
I am worthy of wealth, aligned with purpose, and equipped for legacy.
I am ASCENDing — into prosperity, abundance, and the fullness of who I was created to be.

About the Author

Dr. Juanita Taylor

Dr. Juanita Taylor is a children and adult dentist, entrepreneur, and transformational financial coach who turned her own season of financial struggle into a movement of empowerment for women. After building multiple dental practices and facing overwhelming debt, Dr. Taylor experienced firsthand the weight of financial stress behind the appearance of success. Choosing faith and resilience over defeat, she realigned her income with her purpose and discovered the principles that would become the ASCEND Coaching Framework.

As the creator of the ASCEND program and the author of ASCEND: From Paycheck to Prosperity: The Journey from Financial Stress and Struggle to Financial Freedom and Abundance, Dr. Taylor equips women to rise above financial stress, silence shame and guilt, and step into clarity, confidence, and control. Known as the "Doctor of Prosperity," she blends her professional expertise with her personal journey to guide women in designing lives of freedom, peace, and abundance.

When she's not coaching or writing, Dr. Taylor speaks at conferences, leads workshops, and mentors women who are ready to rewrite their financial stories. Her mission is clear: to help women move from paycheck to prosperity and leave a legacy of purpose, power, and peace.

www.ingramcontent.com/pod-product-compliance
Lightning Source LLC
LaVergne TN
LVHW022041200926
848481LV00003B/732
* 9 7 9 8 8 9 9 8 7 9 0 1 2 *